Thule Explorer
Kayaking North of 77 Degrees

Rosemary Clewes

First Edition

Published by
Hidden Brook Press
writers@hiddenbrookpress.com
www.hiddenbrookpress.com

Thule Explorer
Kayaking North of 77 Degrees

by Rosemary Clewes

Editor - Allan Briesmaster
Cover Art - Rosemary Clewes
Cover Design - Paddy Duncan
Map - Paddy Duncan
Layout and Design - Richard M. Grove

Typeset in Garamond

Printed and bound in USA

Library and Archives Canada Cataloguing in Publication

Clewes, Rosemary, 1935-
Thule explorer : kayaking north of 77 degrees / Rosemary Clewes.

Poems.
ISBN 978-1-897475-05-8

I. Title.

PS8605.L543T48 2008 C811'.6 C2008-900876-6

INGLEFIELD FJORD

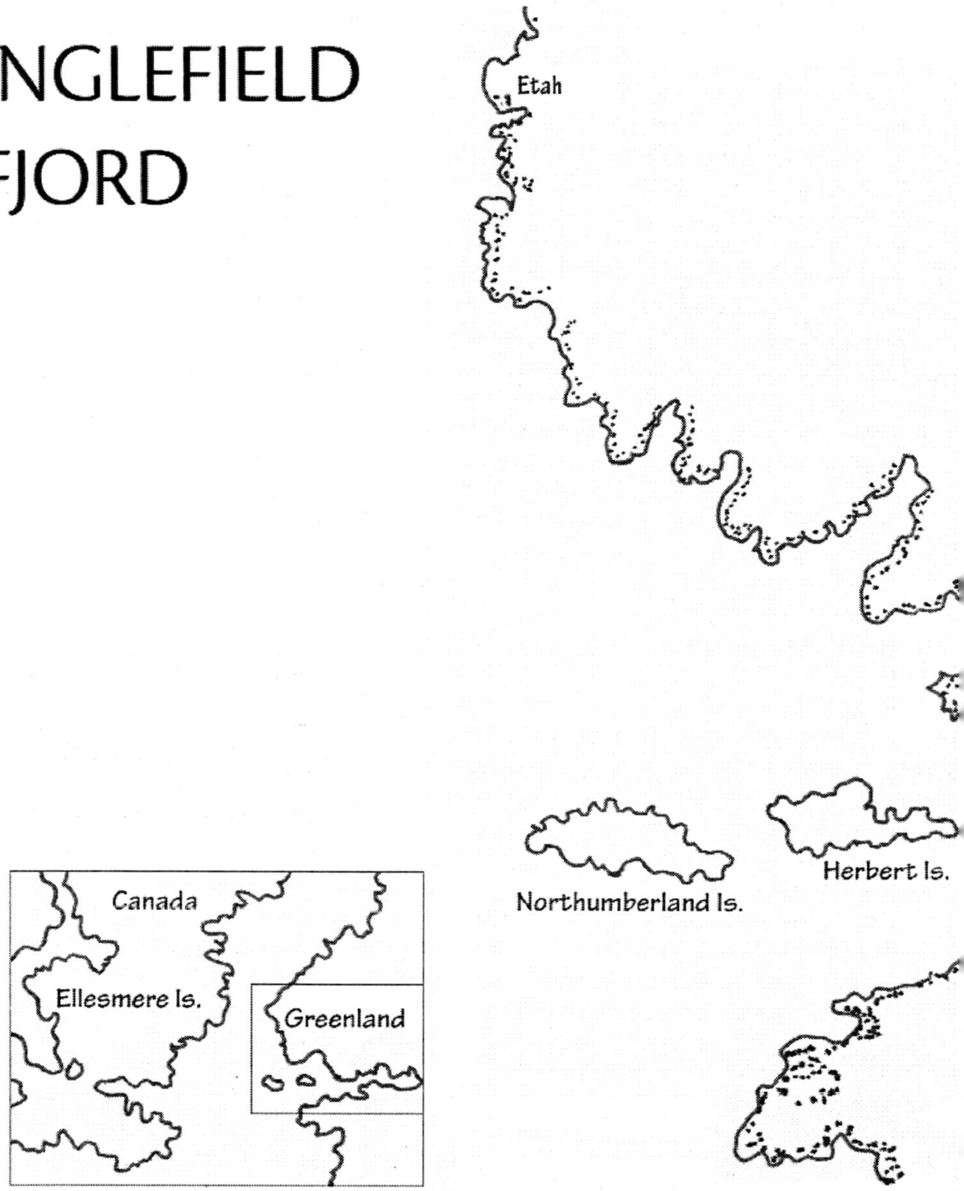

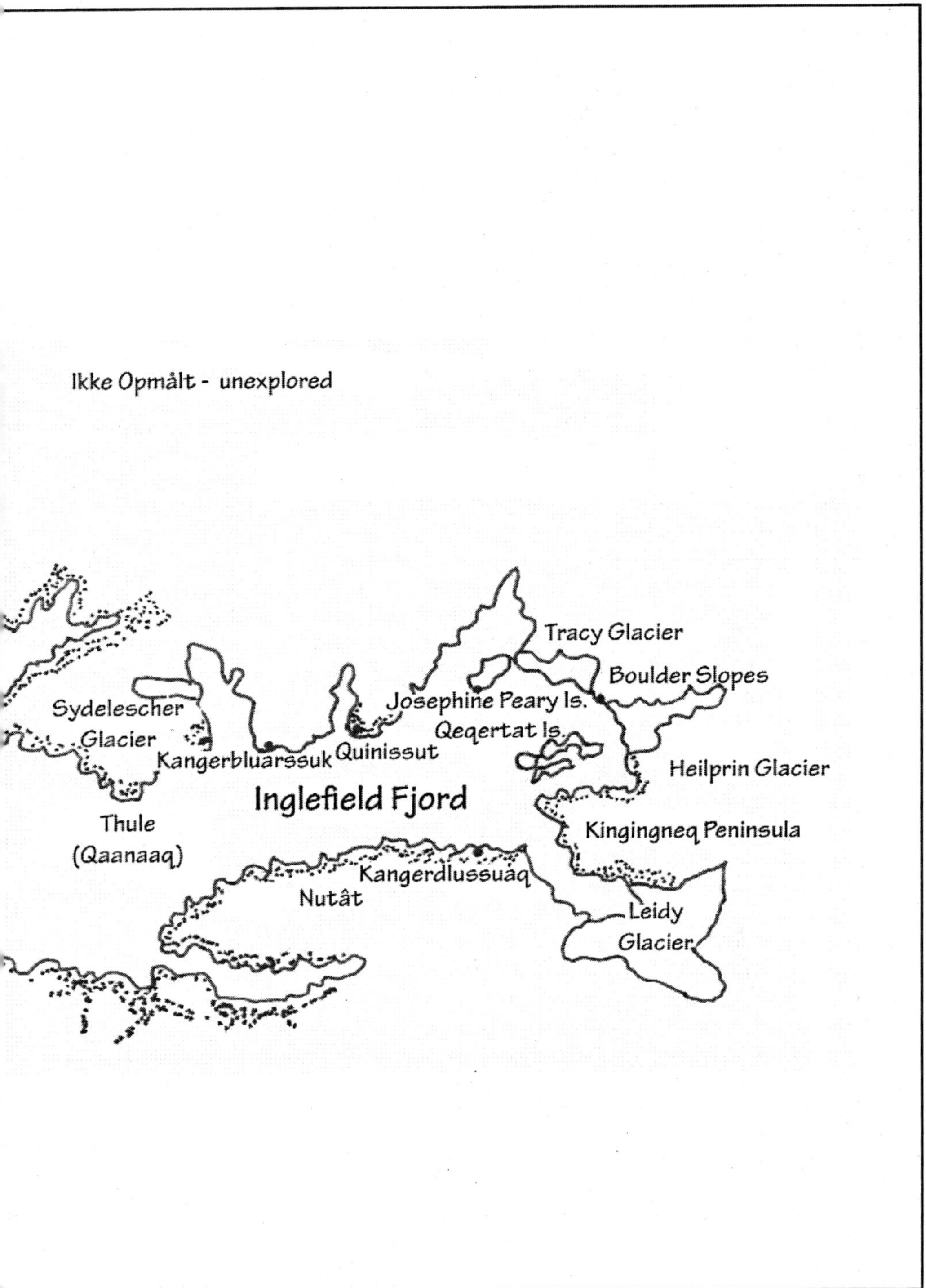
Ikke Opmålt - unexplored
Tracy Glacier
Boulder Slopes
Sydelescher Glacier
Josephine Peary Is.
Qeqertat Is.
Kangerbluarssuk
Quinissut
Heilprin Glacier
Inglefield Fjord
Thule (Qaanaaq)
Kingingneq Peninsula
Kangerdlussuaq
Nutât
Leidy Glacier

Contents

Prologue

I have travelled for a decade in many parts of the Arctic, by ship, raft, and now by kayak. In the first two instances, I encountered empty landscapes, lit as far as the eye could see with the tender summer light. They felt timeless and tranquil, lush, yet austere: landscapes where the relationships between growing things and the activities of animals, and to light and water, soil and ice, seemed harmonious and undisturbed.

To be sure, I saw traces of human presence in the tent rings of stone set high on a tundra plain above a river canyon, or in tombstones marking the ghastly end of explorers' dreams on the deserted beach at Beechy Island.

When the world of Inuit and landscape came together in northwest Greenland, I was grateful for the Arctic primer of earlier summers, and while I had touched the land there, with my hands and feet, I found, travelling under my own steam at a paddling-pace in the Inglefield Fjord, that this realm of ice and flowers was more knowable and accessible.

Kayaking in Greenland, 2002, the land is close-up and intimate. We take each day as it comes, leaving our clocks behind, all proof of our identity left in the storage room in Qaanaaq; and, as nearly as we can, we tread with light feet. We cling to each other yet at the same time grow taller with the thrill of elbow room for the soul, which such infinite space permits. We eat three times in any twenty-four hour period, our days lengthening as the midnight sun rolls them over differently, aligning our internal clocks now to the rhythm of light. We eat later and sleep less, living closer to the Inuit way. Hunters invite us into their summer hunting camps to share a pot of tea and to witness the traditional narwhal hunt by kayak and harpoon. The land lives in these people, and I feel more alive because of it.

What keeps drawing me north is more complex than merely doting on the stripped beauty of land and ice forms. There, I let my eye roam, free of barriers. Indeed, to re-learn the thrill of sight and sound and to ponder them all over again. The surprising vibrancy of tundra brings me to my knees. The drop of dew on a wintergreen leaf has its own way of speaking of mortality.

Many times over the last five years I had thought this book was finished, but whenever I returned to it I found I had more to say. Each additional re-write seemed like the quarter turn given a bottle of wine to bring it to full maturity.

It occurs to me that, as it has ripened, so have I. And further, that the Arctic does not dole out its gifts, gratis. I have worked for them – earned them if you will. The Polar North always keeps one fist behind its back. It gives and it takes, but while full of surprises, it never lies. Learning the land is incremental, and when my understanding falters I return to what I can grasp: a lemon poppy whipped by the wind on a springing stem. Life going on for it: for us all.

Points to Elsewhere

Rain, the size of hailstones, drums against the sides of the plane. We bank over the gravel-grey shore and dive through the roof of cloud. Only a splash of red redeems the gloom. Whitecaps lacing the sides of a red tanker, anchored in last year's sea ice, buoy up the scene. The light's demi-quaver flattens me.

Welcome to Resolute Bay on Cornwallis Island in the east Arctic, temperature, seven degrees Celsius: windsock bursting its seams. People just shrug when Resolute Bay and weather are mentioned in the same breath. The elements are highly unpredictable. Flying in and out (the traveller's only access to this community) is iffy, which is why any statement of intention is followed by a knowing smirk and the mantra "weather permitting." Known as *Qausuittaq*, or Place With No Dawn, this community is a jumping off point to elsewhere for miners, pilots, contract workers and adventurers. Expeditions to the North Pole begin here. We are two groups of eight kayakers, and will fly out on separate trips tomorrow: one group to Ellesmere Island, and mine to the northwest coast of Greenland. Weather permitting.

What follows is the ritual of every group I have ever travelled with. We gather for the first time in the airport, recognizing each other by our heavy jackets and backpacks. Rapid introductions follow, as each of us wags our tails and sniffs out those we think we will like best, making snap judgments that have more to do with the need to be seen as a good team member, than being loveable: measuring our expertise against the others'.

Our guides Dave and Morgan have flown up north with us. We three are Canadian, the rest, American. In this aggregate of ten, for such is what we represent at the moment, there's a much younger Shanna and her husband big Al, who is loaded like a pro under the weight of his cameras. They come from New Mexico and are seasoned kayakers. J. Kent and Mary Nan from Boston, of similar, wiry build, look like peas out of the same pod, making their fifteenth trip to the Arctic. Harold, with the sparkle of an Einstein in his eye, is grinning from ear to ear. I estimate he's in his mid-seventies (making him older than me, thank heavens) and a mathematician from Rhode Island. Dick is short and strong, with a good back for lifting kayaks. He's a developer from Illinois. The dark horse on the trip is Gail from New York, and my tent-mate, who offers little beyond her name, unable to join in the party spirit. Dave and I have already met on the plane. Serene with fine grey eyes is what I noticed. Morgan is too busy with baggage to meet us at the moment.

The South Camp Inn is warm after the bluster. We drop our gear in the lounge and Ozzie, our host, steers us to the dining room for a hot lunch.

We'll re-pack our kit into kayak-size stuff sacks this afternoon for our fourteen-day kayaking trip around the Inglefield Fjord, Greenland. Lon. 69° 19' W, Lat. 77° 29' N.

Sleeping bags, mattresses, woolly hats, hiking boots, Gore-Tex outwear and thermal underwear litter the floor in the lounge. Dave advises us tactfully what to leave behind. One fellow has brought twelve pairs of underwear, another, a dozen books. Didn't they read the equipment list? When a third asks Dave how to pack his cigarettes, I grin, glad these three guys are not travelling with us. Dave is tactful. "I'm not sure I can help you with that."

Meanwhile ropes of rain streak the length of the windowpanes, as the gale batters the walls. Why would anyone choose to live in this gravel pit? Ozzie doesn't miss a beat. He quips, "Someone told me that if I came, I could find a wife behind every tree. Haven't found one yet and I've been here twenty-four years."

It never used to rain in Resolute Bay. This is a new phenomenon in the Arctic, associated with warming temperatures. Weather's howl today makes it easier to imagine this terra incognita (or unknown land) before inhabitants set foot on it. What is the dark mood, the mute depression I sense coming from the drab, unpainted houses? Resolute Bay feels to me like a deserted village, beginning with the limp green sprawl of the oldest buildings at the airport.

Of course there is an official version, telling of Resolute Bay's ignominious dawn, but every member of the seven families chosen to safeguard Canada's northern border has his or her own private stories too. After a long silence and time for the community to regain its balance, these are being told now by the women. They are as dark as any Eskimo tale.

Resolute Bay was named after the ship *H.M.S. Resolute*, sent by the British to search for the lost Franklin expedition in the mid-nineteenth century. Thus, it was just a name on a map before the Canadian Government chose this harsh and forbidding place for The High Arctic Relocation Project in 1953. The world was in the grip of the Cold War and the American Government was beefing up personnel at the Thule base in Greenland, just seventy miles east, across Baffin Bay. The Canadian Government decided that an Eskimo presence was required.

"They divided the families like dogs."

The families were selected as a small experiment from Port Harrison in northern Quebec, an established community consisting of a school, a nursing station, a Royal Canadian Mounted Police Barracks and the Hudson's Bay Trading Post. Eskimos lived on the land, but they used the Hudson's Bay to buy tea and flour in return for skins. Carvings brought in good money. Fish and seal were plenteous. They did not want to go, but as one survivor recalled in the National Film Board video entitled *Broken Promises*, filmed in 1995,

"We were obedient like small children. The government promised abundance of food and (that) we could return in two years."

On July 25, 1953, the families were loaded onto the ship *C.D. Howe* and set out for Resolute Bay and Grisle Fjord, wearing a new issue of short socks and thin parkas. An eighty year old woman, one pregnant woman and a polio survivor had been selected as part of the group.

Most of the Eskimos could not read a map and, that the trip by ship was seventeen hundred miles long, could only be measured by the increasing pack ice and the descending temperatures. They were not told that Resolute Bay was a frozen waste in winter. Seventeen days into the journey, the R.C.M.P. wired the Canadian Government warning them that there were not sufficient animals to sustain life, but the government chose to stick to its plan.

The ship drops anchor, some distance from the wide bay's barren shore. Inland, low hills unfold into more of the same. Wind and the waves' repetitious hiss, perhaps not unlike today, break the awful silence, while nothing moves except the ice rubbing shoulders in the tide. Surrounded by packing crates, the Eskimos watch as the ship sails out of sight, before erecting canvas tents, their only shelter now. They had not been permitted to bring their dogs or sleds for hunting.

"We wondered if we had been placed here to die."

This summation is expressed forty years later without any hostility, after enduring the longest survival story the North has to tell.

On October 14, 1953, the first report arrived back in Ottawa, stating that the Eskimos were *living in canvas tents pitched in blowing snow and burning packing crates for warmth*. Whereas in the more temperate climate of Quebec there had been an abundance of fish and land-game, in the High Arctic there were fewer animals to hunt. If animals did not appear, starvation followed. The Eskimos were accustomed to winter hunting in open water, because the ocean did not freeze over, but far from their homeland, they had to wait in sub-zero darkness beside a seal-hole on the slim chance they could kill a seal.

In 1955, the government acknowledged that *the preservation of Eskimos in their traditional state is not considered feasible*, and offered them a return passage if they could pay for it. In the 1960's a military base was established and with it came alcohol.

"You had to be a tough kid to grow up in Resolute," stated one woman, remembering how the children ran away from drunken parents. "Sometimes one house'd be full of kids ... we couldn't work the heaters. Everyone was freezing. We lost our language, were scared most of the time." Whites were off limits to the Eskimos and she continued, "at night the men from the base'd bring booze and womanized." It wasn't until the 1970's that the bar was shut and the people began to take back control of their lives.

"In a nutshell ... Resolute was a small, isolated, fake community."

The content of stories reflects the values of the age, writes Noah Richler in *This Is My Country, What's Yours?* I want to say that in the fifties, we were all complicit. Class bias was strong and those who weren't of British origin were suspect – Japanese, Italians, Jews and Aboriginals. Reports on the Eskimos could not compete with news on the Cold War, or a decade later, the landing on the Moon. There was still much romantic and condescending babble about the *noble savage.*

I'm haunted by the memory, in the 1940's, of Indians from the reservation in Port Carling, Muskoka, knocking on the back doors of summer cottages to sell their hand woven, sweet grass baskets for just twenty-five cents. They came and went like fragrant shadows in the summer heat.

As a small child, I had no words for those shadows, but they have inhabited my mind like a lingering secret. Beside the deep tree-shade, another more opaque shadow overlay the first and gathered strength in me. For the Eskimo families, a story is growing out of the silence. The women's lips begin to move. "They divided the families like dogs," they tell us again, and the waves go on changing places, as the slit wrist of memory releases another sigh.

Now that I have joined my voice with theirs, I hope I do not stray too far off the map in telling a story which is not my own. With the weight of passivity and memory lifting and healing the past, I question if my assessment of Resolute Bay is even close – Resolute, whose spirit I believed to be broken at the beginning and which continues to feel so to me now.

Resolute Bay has seen it all: the promises from 1953 which were never honoured, opportunists dropping huge tips for charters and a few days hunting, too many outsiders and even adventurers like myself just fly in and out. People rarely stay but return to a more lucrative, comfortable life in the south.

Later, when the rain abates, but not the stinging wind, we hike to the end of town. What catches my eye, as I walk out the door of the South Camp Inn, are the monolithic tanks of oil by the shore, dwarfing the slender white crosses of the cemetery and the subterranean ruins of Thule houses. Oil tanks, the symbolic standing stones of the modern north, hold the sky down to size.

The Weight of a Bird

I get to sit in the first row of the Twin Otter, our charter flight to Greenland. I like this because I can watch the pilots twiddling the bank of dials on the dash, keeping track of knots, altitude and vertical speed.

I wonder if the one that says *Torque* refers to some exotic flying manoeuvre. Their hands rarely stop making minute adjustments to the stick, and from time to time they check the navigational map clipped between them.

The blonde co-pilot and the about-to-be-retired one from Ottawa wear blue overalls. Though I can't hear the music in their headsets, feet in sneakers and boots tap-tap to the same beat. No loo or snacks for the next three hours on this route. I settle for the view. The plane climbs to nine thousand feet.

As we pull away from Ellesmere Island's east shore,
Baffin Bay's shallows waver off rocky beaches.
In mid-sea, snowflakes the size of countries
look too delicate from where I sit
to hold even the weight of a bird,
but currents draw curvy lines
between them in the ink-black water. Surely
it's the pen in the hand of the ice calligrapher
writing summer greetings for the clouds to read.

This is what I have come for.
The Arctic's austere sprawl of rock and water,
dressed up by ice's fanciful transmutations.

Our group of ten arrives in Qaanaaq, in the District of Avanersuaq, which means *Place of the Farthest North*. Qaanaaq is the most northern and largest town of any size on the north-west coast of Greenland. We swing down the ladder of the twin otter and catch our gear as it's off-loaded, piling it on the ground.

Icy air coats my lungs.
Inside my ear, a breeze,
and I know for a cold fact,
there's nowhere else I'd rather be
listening, to sky listening to
                                        earth-stillness –
'til seabirds drawing arcs shake loose the dream,
ratchet up the silence. I count seven glaciers,
angel ice pans rowing their white souls in the grey sea.
Not much here
for wind to flutter or wave.
The play on this stage never begins.
Sometimes the sets fall down,
then restive ice resumes stasis. I stop figuring
and like a child start counting toes –
sky, water, rock/soil, ice.

Hans Jensen, who owns the Qaanaaq Hotel where we will stay for two nights, has come to meet us in his van and trailer. I like his sparkling eyes as he shakes our hands. He has brought with him the immigration officer, a tall, gloomy Dane who, I later learn, wishes he were still in Denmark. It seems they had set out from town, which is only a mile away, when they heard a plane arriving. There aren't that many landing, so they knew it was us. He solemnly ink-stamps, signs and dates our passports by hand. No doubt that I am here, when my passport officially reads *Politiet Qaanaaq*, 8/8-02/MI. Could he have gotten the date wrong? It is August 9 by my reckoning; or am I already slipping out of real time here, where day and night are interchangeable under the midnight sun?

We fold our bodies into the van and bounce along the dirt road into town. No signage distinguishes Hans' hotel from other buildings. It's just a bit longer than those of his neighbours and painted brick red. Cozy double rooms and a shared bathroom lead off the hallway on the back of the building. The dining room windows overlook the fjord we just flew over, its overcast calm dotted with ice. Beyond, the view to the open sea is blocked by Herbert Island (*Qeqertarssuaq*) and Steensby Land, which I couldn't identify as we flew in: each a mountainous arm, guarding the entrance to the fjord, like two rock lions. Five glaciers sweep down from under the ice cap's snowy lid.

Hans' ample wife Birthe, I am told, cooks wonderful casseroles, and in the mornings lays out a Danish-style breakfast of cheese, ham, and bread. Her grandfather, Qavigarssuaq, was a member of the explorer Knud Rasmussen's Fifth Arctic Expedition. In 1921, Rasmussen and Peter Freuchen travelled by dogsled from Greenland to Nome, Alaska, following the migration trail to Greenland the Eskimos had taken across the polar north. They lived in villages for weeks at a time, writing down stories by hand. From these records, we have the first accounts of an ice age culture, unchanged for thousands of years.

I'm settled in my twin room with Gail and head out alone to reconnoitre the town. The streets are empty as I wind down the hill to the shore. Tourists, just beached by a Russian icebreaker, crowd around the doors of the museum and craft shop. Beside the Co-op, a guide is leading the anoraked and curious up the hill to take pictures of a signpost reading, *Nordpolen 1393 Kil.*

Like other Danish towns in Greenland, the houses are painted in primary colours, electrifying the sandbox setting. Hans tells me that Inuit – meaning *Great People* in Greenlandic – can level a space and plunk down a house anywhere he wants. No one owns land. The town's grader, imported from Denmark, keeps the houses connected on the snaky road and ensures that Qaanaaq doesn't slide into the fjord after a tough winter. Two dry gullies slice the town in thirds from top to bottom. In spring they swell with torrents tearing madly from the icecap to the shore. The kids love it when the footbridges between the gullies' banks are washed out and they can leap across the flood without being swept out to sea.

There is a faded red house with pretty lace curtains at the window and another one with a collection of hunting tools and a storm lantern hanging on a blue exterior wall. Unfenced front yards catch the confused overflow of leftover building materials and kids' toys. I give a wide berth to *qinneq* (dogs) staked out on long ropes. They lie curled up, noses tucked under their tails, snoozing away the summer months until freeze-up puts them back to work. The pups run free, but stick close to their mothers.

Boys are pitching stones into the culvert, and only their yips break the town's sleepy mien.

Town Life Revealed

Hans Jensen, it seems, is the busiest man in town, and carries the keys to the Craft Shop, Museum and the Municipal Centre. It's Friday morning and Hans unlocks the Museum for us. The simple building remains unchanged from the days when Knut Rasmussen built it as a home for himself in Dundas village, where the American Thule Air Base is today. In 1910 he established an Arctic trading station there as a base for five expeditions. The house was transported with the rest of the village when it was moved north to Qaanaaq in 1984.

The soft amber lighting of the Museum creates just the right atmosphere for the carefully labelled artifacts in glass cases. Hung on the walls are photographs of Inuit posing after a successful hunt, their faces looking out with a hint of bewilderment and pride. I'm moved by their unsmiling formality, captured in their best clothes for this special photographic record.

One man's haggard face disturbs me. *Mahiautsiag* lived from 1844 to 1910. The plaque reads: "*Angakok* (shaman) aged 65.

"Responsible for an occasional murder to rid the group of a menace – really an execution. The oldest in the tribe, he decided how to rid the community of the person. Murder took place within the context of a daily life situation. This local justice found its natural, although harsh, balance."

A table supports a block of meteorite, so heavy I can't even budge it.

Ten of us crowd around the display cases, unzipping in the sudden heat of indoors, and pelt Hans with questions about the tools of a thousand years ago. It seems implausible to me that without a wood supply, Eskimos could have carved bows and arrows. We argued about that last night at the Thule site in Resolute Bay, but a caribou bone made into a bow lies here under glass and settles the question once and for all.

The marginal existence of life in the Arctic comes home to me as we discuss that first migration across the ice or land bridge from Siberia. Tracking muskox in small groups, Paleo-eskimos drifted east by land to Ellesmere Island about 2500 B.C. They had no knowledge of seafaring or shaping boats, and by 1500 B.C., they disappear, leaving the slate blank for 400 years.

The Dorset people pick up the thread of migration and trekking east, and rule the Arctic for the next 500 years. It's possible that climate or good hunting made life easier for them because they left behind more art than tools. Carving walrus tusks, flint and bone, they articulated the oneness of their world in miniature, human-animal spirits.

On the rafter over my head the smooth underbelly of a sealskin kayak with long raked ends catches my eye. The kayak hasn't changed much and the Dorset must have used one quite like this to hunt whale and walrus. On a plinth by the far wall, walrus tusks, two feet long, gleam in the warm light. Walrus, I'm told, are more dangerous than polar bears. A walrus the size of a small car and armed with swords must be viewed from a sensible distance. Kayakers always paddle close together lest a rogue male try to pick off a *weak* member of the group, but we won't meet one of them on this trip because their habitat is along the east coast of Ellesmere Island.

The next wave of migrants to come to Greenland were truly seafaring. By 1200 A.D., the Dorset either died or intermarried with the Thule people. These brought with them sinew-backed bows, kayaks, *umiaks* (row boats) and dog teams. They hunted caribou and made clothing from skins just as the Inuit do today. In the late 1400's, the Little Ice Age drove most of them south, and once again the landscape was emptied. The Inuit who live in Qaanaaq today are descendants of these people.

The last Thule migration was led by the wily shaman Qitdlarssuag (or Qitdlaq), a strong leader who did not hesitate to kill his rivals. In 1853 he left Baffin Island with a band of followers on a journey north over Devon and Ellesmere Islands. After nine contentious years, a splinter group crossed the frozen Sound and reached their destination in northwest Greenland.

They dug their houses out of whatever soil they could find above the permafrost, using whalebone for low rafters, which were then covered in skins and sod to complete the roof. Last night in Resolute Bay, we explored some grassed-in subterranean houses while we shivered in the lashing wind.

Our next stop with Hans is the Craft Shop, now restocked after the departure of yesterday's cruise ship. I'm looking for a carving with a story, and when I find one, it couldn't be uglier. A male figure carved from caribou bone and 5 inches tall balances on splayed feet. His thick tail tapers to a point behind him and his out-sized square head is more cavity than flesh. Where the heart should be is a hole. Skeletal fingers of one hand curve around genitals, the other hand coasts down his thigh.

Hans calls this carving a *Tupilak*. "The Tuplilak is a man-made creature and very potent. Its mission is to find and kill an enemy," he tells me. The figure pre-dates *qallunaaq* (white man) and when Danish colonizers reached Ammassalik, on Greenland's east coast, in 1884, the Greenlanders carved replicas for them, and since then, the Tupilak has become popular as folk art.

A shaman or his apprentice would patch together animal parts – bone, skin, teeth, claws, beaks, skulls and bits of turf while singing a magic song. If hair or nails from the victim could be included, so much the better. This took several days and when it was finished, the shaman sat astride the piece, rubbing his penis against it and singing. When the Tupilak shivered into life, he would conceal it in a river or the sea to track and kill his victim. This carried a risk. If the intended victim was more powerful than the maker, the Tupilak would return to kill him. With a twinkle in his eye, Hans teases me. "Don't give it to anyone you don't like." I hope the carver, whose imagination is still fired by the old beliefs, has not already cast a spell on it.

The Co-op jolts me out of history and spell-making back to reality. There's enough square footage in this metal-sided barn to supply a city, or so it seems. Liquor, food, pharmaceuticals, toys, junk food, pop, racy videos, boots, jackets, and guns fill the shelves, with big bulk items ending up at the ends of aisles on the floor. Why should I be surprised that all the vices and virtues of the south can be had here for a few kroner? The girls streak their hair crimson and boys wear their caps backward.

My view of the town is turned upside down by the The Municipal Centre. I never guessed with my outsider's eyes that Qaanaaq is so well connected to the world, and as Hans whisks us along a hallway of offices, I peek in and see an Inuit behind every screen. The place is humming. He shows us an elegant meeting room with a long polished table. The soft green walls show off a stunning polar bear pelt.

Today's modern Greenlander spends more time in meetings than in hunting camps. Hans tells us that Greenland, as part of Denmark, joined the European Union, but then withdrew in 1985. Now it is self-governing with Nuuk, in the south, as its capitol. However, the movement for complete sovereignty remains weak while supplies and many services are still subsidized by Denmark.

Back at the hotel I meet a lanky Dane and a German photographer who tell me that a research project mounted by Denmark is underway using our hotel as a base. Every day, weather permitting, they fly over the fjords counting narwhal, the shy and elusive black whale with a long ivory tusk found only in polar waters.

The Danes strafe the surface with thousands of shots from a Haselblaad camera mounted in the floor of the plane. When I ask them about the whales under the surface, they just shrug and smile. They don't care about the numbers. Nonetheless the calculation, conducted at great cost to the Danish government, will be the basis for new policy. A quota will be placed on hunting. What is the evidence that there is over-hunting at the present time? What will be lost?

Greenlanders participate actively in the North West Greenland Hunters Association and are the envy of their Canadian counterparts, who depend on skidoos and motorboats and the all too frequent government subsidies to re-fuel them. Here they are carefully balancing Denmark's largesse against the *old ways* in order to keep their culture vibrant. Traditions weigh lighter on the scale today, and who can blame them for preferring the ease and comfort which health clinics, schools and a ready supply of imported food in the Co-Op brings them. Those who hunt are still proud of their skills, but the hardship and starvation of the past is over.

Are You Up To This?

After a sumptuous lunch laid out in the dining room by Birthe, we pack, storing what we're not taking with us in a common duffle. I tick off in my mind the comforts I'll be leaving behind: the last hot shower; the last sit-down pee; the support of chairs and the warmth of the hotel. I've been eyeing the far shore where we'll be camping tonight, and I see misted-out mountains and glaciers looking glum under a sagging sky. Five boats have been hired to take us the fifteen miles across open water to Nutak, an Inuit camping site on the south side of the Inglefield Fjord.

From there we'll follow the fjord's shoreline, keeping it on our right all the way, until we arrive back at Qaanaaq twelve days later. I trudge down the road in my Wellingtons to where the Inuit are lashing our kayaks onto the decks of boats. One fellow stands out, as he lolls against the hull of a beached boat trailing a cigarette from his tapered fingers. He's as bright as a Christmas cracker in his red, blue and white striped toque and florescent lime-green wind pants. Right down to the orange tips of his Wellies he has the look of a typical Inuit hunter, with his elegant, tight build. The rheumy eyes of an old man in such a strong body take me by surprise. He nods sweetly when I ask if I can take his picture, adjusting his view seaward.

Dressed in our warmest, Harold and I settle for the long ride in the middle seat. Our young boatman stands facing the bow and us, and like a Newfoundland fishermen, grasps the long tiller behind him and bends into the wind. His rubber overalls balloon around his skinny frame, knees absorbing the neck-jarring smack of the bow as it slams over every wave. I try turning my face into the wind but can't take it. Tears stand in his eyes, his nose is reddened and pinched with the cold, yet he never flinches. In mid-fjord he detects a glitch in the motor which I can't hear and stops it, plunging his hand into the icy water to adjust the exhaust system. His father, who is driving the boat ahead, waits for us.

I like our boatman's sweet face, but when he smiles, I notice his teeth are decayed. He tells me he is twenty-six years old. His father, he adds, is an old man. When I ask how old, he tells me fifty-one years. I laugh and say Harold and I are much older. He has strapped his own kayak on the deck beside ours, because after he drops us at Nutak, he'll continue down the fjord to hunt narwhal.

Talking takes too much effort in the wind, so I daydream. Pictures hover in my mind of sleeping in fourteen degrees Celsius tonight. Will I be warm enough if I cinch the hood of my new sleeping bag around my head? In the morning I'll hobble out of the tent for breakfast after a night spent a foot or two above the permafrost. Bold print flashes in front of my eyes, **Are you up to this?** But I dismiss nervous Nellie's voice with a shrug, telling her it's too late now.

I relax when a dull green apron of land begins to open up like a welcome mat. Tundra. Hooray! This isn't the first time I've camped on this lumpy mix of rocks, wildflowers and grasses: the Arctic version of a meadow. My anxiety slides down a notch.

The downside of this trip is that I have to share a tent. On rafting trips in British Columbia and the Yukon, I've rented my own because there's room for extra stuff on a raft. These tents are tight for two and it helps to laugh a lot, but my tent mate Gail is as humourless as the weather. When I ask her what she does, she briefly explains that she paints theatre sets, once for the Metropolitan Opera, but offers nothing more after that.

We arrive at Nutak together and disembark. I nip up the hill ahead of her and choose a more-or-less level place for the tent near the designated kitchen. What an odd team we make as we thread the poles through the loops, with a nod and a yup from me just to keep things going. The tent snaps open and we peg it down.

Now I can explore that ribbon of sand I saw as we approached the camp. I noticed how it wound smoothly between the seal-black water and the cliffs. I've an hour before supper and, like a puppy just let off the leash, I lope along the sand, eager to be alone, wading in the frigid water to test the inch-thick liners of my boots. High overhead, blocky boulders balance precariously on precipitous scree slopes. God's little finger could topple them in a thunderous freefall, but for the moment gravity holds them in suspension. How could something the delicious colour of lumpy brown sugar have any designs on me?

I look up at the scalloped outline of the icecap overhanging the cliffs. A stream of glacial melt is splattering over descending ledges, echoing between the walls of a recessed gully. I dip my fingers in a clear pool and they numb in seconds. Fresh water 10,000 years old.

Each time I come to a curve in the beach I look back to see if I'm out of sight of our camp yet, and try on the idea that I am all alone, self-reliant and fearless. To tell the truth, I'm envious of the lone boatman hunting for narwhal somewhere down the fjord. The idea thrills and terrifies me.

Before bed, Dave gives us the scoop on bathroom rules. The tundra beyond our tents peters out into pink boulders the size of tables, then dips into a hidden gulley out of which the glacier's outflow tumbles into the fjord. This is the open tap for drinking water, washing and bathroom needs. We do not have many rules, but about this Dave is specific. Toilet paper will not break down, so don't use it. Go to the bathroom below the tide line, wash and take your drinking water from above. If a campsite doesn't have fresh water, there's nothing as sterile as the salty ocean. I love the simplicity and I puddle around in the gushing creek squatting to do my teeth, just listening. Somehow it doesn't matter anymore what the weather does. Qaanaaq's comforts have no claim on me now as I dawdle like a shorebird on a holiday.

I peck around the bergy bits, which are hunks of old ice one to five metres tall. The tide heaves them up on shore for a day or two and then reclaims them. Off they sail again, shrinking daily on a journey to slow death. While they wait for release, they weep in the warm air. This one in front of me, planted in the sand, looks like a frozen wave, or a wedge of wind arrested and pressed into a dripping mould. It draws me into the sapphire cave of its belly. A shoulder blade arcing out of one hip, or perhaps the starched flare of a nun's wimple, will be the next casualty. Edges of frazzled lace contest gravity, and as I tip my ear to catch a chorus of drips, I hear the forest in my head shaking out its leaves after a long rain.

Narwhal Watch

Mystery still surrounds *Mondon monoceros*, the narwhal whose creamy spiraled horn grows a tusk like a giant tooth out of the left side of the male's lip. From nine to twelve feet in length and anywhere from eight to ten pounds in the hand, it measures about one third the total size of this small whale. Before the seventeenth century it was believed that the horn belonged to the mythical unicorn, and one elaborately jewelled tusk hung in every collection of a European royal.

Science can't tell us what these dark knights of the ocean use their tusks for. Some believe the narwhal forage with it on the sea floor for food. Sparring males have been seen to cross their tusks like two swords while they rest their heads above the water. Others believe the tusk is for sexual display.

Typically, in the oral tradition of the Eskimos – the ancestors of today's Inuit – there was a story to explain every phenomenon. This story has the feel of being outside of time – for all time, if you like, where the metaphor of landscape embodies the meaning. As in a true epic story, there are heroic characters but no heroes. The real story and caution is going on underneath.

This one tells how the narwhal got its tusk.

A very long time ago, a woman and her two grandchildren – a boy and a girl – had left their group. They were starving. The boy, the older child, had been blind from birth. A bear, *nanoq*, came to the *igalaaq* or iglu window. The grandmother told the boy to shoot while she bent the bow and took aim. Then she pretended that they had missed the bear.

The grandmother instructed the little girl to help her drag the bear away so they could eat it nearby. But though sworn to secrecy, the little girl saved food for her brother so that he did not go hungry. One day he asked his sister to lead him to the water because he was thirsty and wanted to drink. Then he sent her away, and while he was sitting by the shore, he heard a great whistling in the air. A huge bird landed beside him and instructed him to hang on to its neck. The boy did this and the bird carried him under the water. This happened four times, when the boy then said that he was beginning to see again.

When his sight returned, the boy made his way back to the iglu. As he entered he told his grandmother that there was a bearskin stretched out on the path. The grandmother lied, telling him that it was a present from Persorssuaq's family.

One day, the boy saw some white whales playing off the shore. He prepared his harpoon, tying the end of the line to his sister's leg. It was believed that the sister would become the 'whale's tail', and if he was successful in killing the whale, she would receive that portion due a hunting partner.

The grandmother begged to be tied too, and so this he did. When the boy killed a whale, she urged him to kill another. A bigger one, she said. But this time, he wounded a great white whale and as it swam away from the shore, the line began to drag on the grandmother's leg. She was holding on to the line for balance and then she grasped the little girl's boot, but when that too failed, the grandmother disappeared under the water. Several times she bobbed to the surface and shouted for her knife, for she hoped to cut herself free. And just as her hair was being braided into a pigtail, she was dragged by the whale down to the bottom of the sea. There she was transformed into a black male narwhal that had a long twisted tusk in its mouth.

This cautionary tale was one of many which, in the telling, upheld the centrality of the group rather than that of the individual, and was typical of Eskimos' explanatory stories that sought to keep order in a community concerned with survival, and where the loyalty of each to each was therefore of prime importance. In this story, the community of three is protected through the co-operative exchange between animals and humans, at the expense of the individual. Good and evil are clearly delineated to drive the point home to those listening. Stories, which reinforced the *allernersuit* (taboos), enabled the group to live in a proper balance with nature. These tales were the first maps to show people how to navigate in a treacherous world.

In the middle of the night before the rain began, I heard outboard motors landing on the shore and this morning woke to find two Inuit families in tents beside ours. I'm delighted with this shared use of land and that outsiders, like us, are treated equally. Greenland's fjords and tall coast are short on level camping sites, and besides, families love to go summer hunting. I'm fascinated and watch them covertly as they drink coffee and go in and out of their tents. We say good morning but otherwise respect our separate spaces.

An Inuk has been glassing the fjord all night watching for narwhal. Inglefield Fjord is a favourite feeding ground for them and the hunters know the whales will stop to graze on halibut, which feed on the mineral-rich waters at the base of the glaciers. The camp has been in use for hundreds of years in this way, providing a good outlook and beach for butchering if they should be successful this morning.

Two featherweight kayaks are cradled on the rocks by the shore now, like wings, ready and open to fly. Their three-dimensional grace unfolds like a graphite drawing rendered simply. The hunters make their own boats out of treated canvas. A neatly coiled rope, a steel-tipped harpoon, an inflated seal bladder and *drogue* (brake) each have their designated position on the deck. A hunter will paddle his kayak within striking range of the oncoming whales, then store his paddle under the lines on the deck, and float, silent as the sea ice until the whales swim into view. The Northwest Greenland Hunters Association enforces a rule that the first strike at a whale must be made with a harpoon from a kayak.

When the harpoon pierces the whale, the rope pays out, taking the float and the drogue with it, leaving the kayak free. The drogue, which looks like a box without a lid, brakes in the water, slowing the whale's flight while the float balloons on the surface to show the hunter its diving path. It may take six or eight strikes to exhaust the whale to a point where the hunters can get right next to it and shoot or lance it. If the hunters are lucky today, they'll bring a narwhal back to the campsite and dress it on the beach.

Suddenly the Inuk on watch starts to yell and the hunt is on. We're so excited we quit packing our kayaks and leap up on the high rocks to follow them with our binoculars. We keep up a running commentary, plying Dave and Morgan with questions. It takes about forty-five minutes for the hunters to reach their positions at the foot of the glacier.

The Hunt

i)

Bending down to brace his weight
upon the paddle's shaft laid flat
between the rocks and slender bow,
he steps inside and sits – the kayak
angled at his hips, his bloodied anorak
and boat the white of soiled ice.

ii)

In the middle of the night the hunters came
and pitched two tents – a watch kept watch
and hollered when he saw the whales swim up-fjord.
They launch two kayaks light as snow, shake loose
the mirrored mountains, passive sky. A harpoon thrown
to test the eye, then stowed upon the deck.
A blizzard of white-clad arms quickens
and the hunters' paddles fly, their gazes fixed
on the glacier's blasted face, invisible
behind the countries made of ice. Their camouflage
complete, white seabirds both and decoy-still,
they idle now, wait the rise and dive of glistening backs,
the synchrony of narwhal. They come
in pods of five. Black arcs. And from the vantage
of the shore their blowing seen as mist. Harpoons drawn,
the hunters poise to kill. No arm release
until the range is right – too cool for false moves.
One pod passes out to sea. The other too.
But later, at another camp, a mighty ton is towed
to shore, first deep cut and crimson spill upon the stones.
A whale is drawn and quartered now, flensers sheathed,
and in the cache of circled rocks the livid meat.

I'm both relieved and disappointed when the hunters let the pod go without a strike. I wanted to see the hunt but not the blood. Don't know what it would be like to watch them tow the whale home and flense it into chunks, the shore and sea turning crimson; its head and guts left to rot on the sand. A half-hour goes by and three more narwhals swim past the hunters, but they've called it quits and spin back to the campsite. One of them glides into shore, balances his paddle on a rock, and standing up in the kayak – something I would never dare to do – steps on to the shore. In one quick move, the canvas skirt, which fastens over the combing of the kayak to keep the paddler dry, drops from around his waist and lands like a stand-up collar at his feet. He steps over the edge then picks it up. I'm so taken with the elegance of this gesture I aim to bring it to perfection with my own spray skirt before going home.

While the hunters carry their kayaks above the tide line, we fly off our perches and land like hungry ravens on the shore to take pictures. I try to find out what happened, stuttering in excitement at the tall, husky one in a white anorak. "Narwhal?" I ask stupidly, pointing toward the glacier and raising my shoulders and eyebrows in question marks. He smiles and utters something in the strange music of Inuktitut, a language full of exploding 'k's' and 'q's' – glottal athletics that swallow the sound in the middle of words.

Now It's Their Turn To Watch Us • We go back to packing kayaks. Three men and a boy wearing a bright yellow T-shirt captioned *American Skate* in blue drift over to our section of the beach and sit down on the rocks by the bank.

There are five red double kayaks with blunt snouts trade-named *Necki Amaruk*, meaning "Sea Wolf" in Inuktitut, lined up on the sand. They look something like a workhorse version of the sexier models with pointy noses we paddle at home. I kneel beside the bow hatch I'm responsible for, surrounded by my stuff sacks, tent, sleeping bag and pelican box for camera, but Dave keeps adding food and kitchen utensils to my pile. Each kayak has to carry its share of grub and all of it must find a place inside the hatches or on deck. I panic when I compare the size of my five stuff sacks to the tiny opening of the hatch in the bow. All are too fat. There's lots of room inside the bulkhead if I can just punch them through the opening.

One by one I untie the drawstrings, unwind three layers of plastic bags used for waterproofing, then walk my knees up and down, making sausage shapes out of them, squeezing out the last trace of air, before twisting them back down. While I'm shoving with all the oomph I can muster, Dave is finishing with the back hatch. He comes over to finish the job for me. "My hands are strong 'cause I'm a carpenter," he says. Just when I think the hatch is full, he adds a bag of apples, a loaf of bread, his sneakers and the ubiquitous duct tape. Our friends on the rocks look amused, full of wonderment and disbelief. We have so much stuff. Finally we buckle the hatches and I turn to my survival suit.

These are one-piece suits, zip-up-the-front style, lined with airtight pockets that keep you afloat if you fall in. They come in three sizes and at 5' 8" and 130 pounds I'm stuck with a 'small'. I try to wrestle it over my hips, but lose my balance and crash to the ground giggling. I pray the hunters have not seen my fall from grace and change strategies. Wellies off now, sitting on a rock I manage the legs, replace my boots, stand up and tug it up like an old fashioned corset, then twist to find the armholes.

Most of us have been prancing about in long underwear, modesty ditched in the interests of comfort; Dick in midnight blue with baggy knees; Harold and Gail in tomato red, ditto knees; Mary Nan and J. Kent, slim, in much-washed orange. Secretly, I'm glad that my long underwear is the forgiving colour of black and the knees are still trim. I zip up and cinch the waist, try lifting my legs and fail.

Dave launches the kayak and, as I fold my limbs awkwardly into the bow, my feet come to rest against clattering pots. He flattens my daypack and squeezes it between my knees, then hands me the rifle to pass to him after he gets settled. Polar bears rarely come to this area in summer, but we carry a gun in case. At last we're buoyant. We turn and wave goodbye to our new friends.

Like skaters we step onto new ice –
kayaks gliding between the solitudes of clouds
  shake out mother-of-pearl V's.
          Ripples return to stillness.

Dave and I settle easily into a paddling rhythm and marvel at cliffs so tall, only birds can get a toehold. Soon, gentler shores open onto tundra and we pull in to camp for our second night. Kangerdlugssuaq, as it's named on the map, slopes gradually to the water, making it easy for our first carry above the tide line. I help put the last kayak down and, straightening up, dig my thumbs into my lower back, easing stiff muscles.

The best camping sites have fresh water and ours has an unstoppable supply. It spews out of the cliff's swollen lip, hammering the creek below in its inexorable rush to the sea.

I dream a dream of winter.

Tauvikjuaaq's heartbeat slows.
The Great Dark ice-fist   clutches
the gutsy torrent by the throat
muzzling the music.
                    Inside your long white sleep,
you draw down the stars to light your brow –
but solid form was nothing you could count on for long
tamed, but a moment
                    before the golden gorge of summer
sets you singing again.

Our first day has been a kind of test run, as we flexed our tenting, packing and paddling muscles. Gray skies or blue, I'm ready for anything.

A Glimpse of the Underglimmer • Dave and Morgan suggest a hike after dinner on the other side of the creek. I zig-step the boulder bank, choosing the driest stone mid-creek, then leaping to the far side. We crest a hill and I'm dumb-struck to see a proper house dropped into a grassy valley, a half-mile below. Open windows invite, yet the house seems reserved in a weather-shaped way. I see it through the eyes of American painter Andrew Wyeth, who would have captured exactly the liquidity of light angling the window sash. He'd have dry-brushed the silvered walls in a single stroke, laying in the pitch and shingle of roof, and each blade of grass rising to my feet.

Hearing the sound of our voices, three hungry pups come rollicking across the grass to beg and nip at our heels. A bitch circles anxiously on her chain, pitching her ears in our direction. Greenlanders like their dogs half wild, feeding them just enough to keep them healthy in summer, thus making them tougher in winter when they may have to travel long stretches without food.

A well-used path leads between the main dwelling and a square sod house close by. The sod house is five feet high, with cracked glass windows and a low door. Once, seal oil lamps lit the windows and a family was warm enough inside these walls rimed with ice. Fifty years ago, Greenlanders stretched sealskin over the windows and laid blocks of turf against the exterior walls for insulation. The blocks are crumbled now and the decaying roof is sprouting grass. Beside the door, a blackened meat cache stands next to a drying rack.

In the tangled grass between the two houses is the usual mess: a broken child's sled, turquoise nylon twine, a paddle, harpoon, whale vertebrae, and a caribou's rack. Ragged sheets of shiny blue plastic lie across rotten boards and the putrid smell of old blubber hardened onto the blackened rocks makes my stomach turn. The soft evening sunshine quarrels with the feeling of abandonment, yet this is the norm, and the owners, who are probably hunting down-fjord, will return to feed their dogs tomorrow or next week.

The debris throws my romantic notions out of kilter. I have seen this in every town on Baffin Island, where the residents heave their junk out the front door or leave it to rot on shores. Summer camp in Ontario taught me to leave a place in better condition than I found it, and what soothes my soul after a surfeit of city walls is a long view without human clutter.

I've read that our agricultural roots are responsible for my pristine preferences, in which quilted fields of crops roll out their colourful patterns between fence lines. I remind myself that the Inuit belong to a hunter-gathering society, until recently nomadic. Land is shared and killing, disposal and consumption are conducted on the spot. When they travel on over the land, they use sky, tides and ice as a bulletin board for survival. Nothing is as beautiful to an Inuit as a seal lying beside its breathing hole after four unsuccessful days of hunting. They spend as much time admiring the mountains as I the skyscrapers in downtown Toronto.

We're ambling around the back of the two-story when we spot a mound of rocks, twenty feet from the back steps. An early Christian grave we guess, because of the encrustation of silver and black lichen, over and in between the spaces, which proves the rocks have not been moved for years. We bend down to look beneath them at the wooden coffin lying in its own deep shadow. A weathered cross, which no one has thought to straighten, tilts in the prevailing wind. We stumble around the grave respectfully sneaking a peek at death between the stones.

When the Inuit were Christianized, they adopted our style of underground burial, yet the permafrost often lies a shallow foot below the surface. Traditionally a body was wrapped in skins placed in a shallow pit and covered with stones. Humans, they thought, had many *anirniit* (souls) and when death came, the souls had to unify before they could leave the body to find another to inhabit.

I remember visiting Tanu in the Queen Charlotte Islands, where Emily Carr once painted. That day I walked with ancestors under the old trees. Those cedar matrons wearing hooped skirts – I would like to have talked to them had I known how – closed ranks like Haida *watchmen*, guarding the perimeter of the village, the fallen foundations and house posts: all traces of life going on erased under a soft blanket of emerald-coloured moss. The graveyard's green velvet soliloquy spoke to me of absence just as this wooden coffin does, but not of abandonment. Nature never abandons it own. The ancient ones are left to watch over its unstoppable reclamation. It helped me then, to get the meaning of *ashes to ashes* ...

I wonder if Inuit souls get to tell their stories when they inhabit a new body. If not, at least Christianity has added a new story about death to the Inuit oral tradition. A small burial ground on top of the hill behind the house grows a white cross on every grave. Was there always enough soil or did they have to haul it up? Plastic flowers in chemical colours adorn the graves like a spring garden planted with the wrong fertilizer. I make a face, figuring that this is one too many imports from the south. But in a landscape with few primary colours, florescence must be heady stuff. Don't paintings with red in them sell faster? In Ontario, the gauzy blue of October sky performing its grace notes over jazzy maple leaves seems just right to me.

Underneath this ersatz embellishment lie fifteen graves in two rows, each a neat rectangle, separated by strips of wood, wedged into the earth: tiny, linear fields celebrating the straight lines of the European God.

I keep thinking about the solitary grave by the house and how it drew me out of this world. For a moment I believed I stood at history's overlap with this soul, and in the words of the wandering pilgrim-poet Basho, "a glimpse of the under-glimmer" opened the door for me to another people, another place and another time.

Where Sky Meets Mountains in the Water

Oqaluttuarpoq! Someone is telling a story! These were the formal words a Greenlandic Inuit spoke before beginning a story. The family lies down on the *illeq*, the sleeping platform in the *iglu*, their heads close together facing the centre. As the soft flame of the *qulliq*, (soapstone lamp), wavers low, it throws their shapes into black relief against the rounded walls and the children settle into the dream-space of story as the teller begins. In the morning, their parents will instruct them in what they do not understand and help them to say some of the difficult sentences and, by repetition, the story will be committed to memory. In the fifties, the people recited a body of some two hundred myths, although only five or six storytellers, both men and women, knew every word by heart.

No one ever interrupts the storyteller, even if he's just telling how he took a seal the night before. His phrases rise and fall in an expressive chant and are as fluid as the reflections bending the cliffs out of shape in front of the kayak this morning.

We are leaving the glassy waters of the Inglefield Fjord and entering the Academy Fjord. A fulmar, skimming the surface, makes a wingtip copy of itself in the shimmer. Water opens its transparent mouth with every paddle stroke, remembering a time of permeable worlds where animals had souls, married and procreated with people.

Oqaluttuarpoq! There was a young girl who did not want to marry. Her father cursed her, saying, "If you did not want to marry, you must marry a dog." That night a handsome stranger with long teeth appeared and took her to wife. The people then removed her to an island where she could live with the dog. Every day the dog returned to the camp to hunt for deer and seal meat for his wife. The girl bore many children, some were human and some were dogs. Now the old man was sorry for his daughter and one day he drowned the dog by weighing his sack of meat with rocks.

The daughter planned her revenge. She told her children to destroy her father's kayak the next time he came to visit, but he was suspicious and escaped. Without meat, her children were starving, and in order to save them, she placed the dog children in the sole of her boot. She made sails out of two blades of grass. They sailed away south and became *qallunaat* or white men. Then the old man took her with her human children back to his house.

One day a tall man appeared in a kayak. The girl hid, but when he called "*Ooeeneegoomashuikukkilik!*", meaning, she who will not be married, she went with him in the boat. She saw that he stood on a stool and wore goggles. When they stopped by an ice floe, he got out and took them off. She began to cry when she saw his red eyes and his short body. He was a *kakoodlak*, a fulmar, also known as "bird of the storm." He begged her not to cry and promised her a tent made of silverjar seals, if she would come with him.

But he was lying, for she found a tent made of fish skins instead. Her father felt sorry for her again, and while the fulmar was hunting, stole her away in his *umiak*, his large skin boat. Kakoodlak flew after them and called out that he wanted his wife back, but she taunted him for his goggles and red eyes.

The bird flew faster and the wind came up, but the father wouldn't give her back. When the waves threatened to capsize the umiak, he threw his daughter overboard to save himself. She clung to the boat, but the father cut off the first joints of her fingers. These turned into *netsek* (ringed seal). He cut off the second joints and these turned to *oogjoo* (bearded seal). The third joints became *aiverk* (walrus). After that, the girl sank. The old man was very sad and rolled himself up in his sleeping skins on the beach. A great wave came and took him into the sea. He sank then, to the bottom where his daughter lives. Now she, *Takanaluk Angaluk*, rules the sea animals and he sleeps next to her and punishes the wrongdoers. The dog husband lies across the door, to keep people out. When the Great Woman is angry she hides all the seals in her house.

And who is *Takanaluk Angaluk* or the same by other names? *Nerrivik* or *Neqivik*? Where did she come from? "It's a story every child knows," writes Jean Malaurie, in conversation with *Pualana*, in *The Last Kings of Thule*. "In the evening, the old women who know everything would tell you the story without leaving out a single word or detail. Go see Amannalik, in Uuminannaq! She talks a lot, but she doesn't lie. ... Have you any tobacco left?"

The sea cliffs have heard this story too, and give me their shadows and walls to lean into. Where sky meets mountain in the water, I paddle on the edge of two worlds.

We can feel the bite of wind
off the glacier before we see it.

Its polar muscle, a tumultuous sky-high
river-fall, bisects
the monotonic mountains;
granite gateway to the shove of ice.

The glacier cliffs out of the fjord
                                        in a ruin,
fists powder blue and bluer-green seracs
into our sea-level-kayak faces.

Halfway up, rock islands blown clean of snow.

I try to guess the reach of this white sky laid low on earth. Who can measure the sky?

The Tango Makes Light Work of Landings • We pull in to our campsite half a mile from the Leidy Glacier. If I thought packing our kayaks after the narwhal hunt was a challenge, levering my body out of the cockpit at the end of a day's paddle is a real test. The steps to this dance are important, but first there's the agony of unhinging my limbs, and wresting the knapsack from between my legs, which has kept me pinned under the combing since lunch.

There is nobody in the whole world
Who dances better than me

boasts the conceited *compadrito* of Buenos Aires, expressing the reigning sentiment of the tango in the 1920's. I claim no such distinction, but the first step begins in a graceful fashion by placing my hands behind me on the deck. Hips rise now to a horizontal plane, accompanied by a slight angling of the profile. Bent knee brings right leg to chest above deck – it's not always the right – then straightening it high above my head, I rotate the ankle. Picture now, a V, revealing the sturdy heel of the Wellington Boot. It is thought that dancing shoes with a higher heel and strap would not suit this particular setting.

You should not expect any help,
Nor favour, nor hand

wails the lonely *portena*, the tango by now a sad and melancholic dance. My partner Dave, spinning me silently through the last steps, now squats beside the kayak, primed for the penultimate moment when our forces conjoin to catapult me from V to vertical. Once sprung from the cockpit, he gallantly releases my arm, steadies me with a touch. Alas, I am unable to follow his lead because my hamstrings are tight as a guitar's bass string, propelling me in free-form-reverse into the last dying steps of the dance.

After this, I trip headlong over a rock, bruising my knee. With a ready supply of ice, I recline on stuff sacks with my leg once again in the air, while the rest of the group enacts the ritual dance of lifting the kayaks above the tide line.

They strip off their yellow suits, preferring their multi-hued long johns, then like good soldiers line up beside the first kayak. It takes eight people to hoist one, three to a side and one at each end. Morgan acts as choreographer, ever watchful of our backs. "One, two three, hup!" They arrow up in unison, then stagger uphill, groaning, straddling boulders and all the spaces in between. It works better when they stay in step but it's every man for himself, just to stay upright. On cue they lower the kayaks along the prominent line of black lichen, a plant which can't survive in salt water and thrives only above the tide line. We don't take any chances.

This funereal-looking inedible lichen, otherwise known as Rock Tripe, helped to prolong the lives of members of the Franklin expedition in 1822.

Real Estate Issues • I begin to get anxious around tent-pitching time. I may not sleep in my tent, but I need to know I have a roof over my head. I wander around looking for even, dry ground. Gail is drawn to moss, which you can wring out like a sponge, but in the end she settles for my choice. Mostly, we sleep on lumpy ground, packs, rolled clothes or boots wadded under legs to prevent the inevitable slide out the door.

I want my home to be a middling distance from others, open front and back to a cross-breeze and properly staked against high winds. We've acres of tundra to spread ourselves out on this evening, with a view of the Leidy Glacier rolling away like an ice-prairie to our left, the fjord at our feet and mountains across the sound.

These real-estate issues are obviously shared by everyone else. Al and Shanna, who live at a celestial elevation in New Mexico, always pitch their tent at the loftiest point on the landscape. They've taken me under their wing and point out the best level spot for Gail and me as they cart their own gear up-mountain. I've noticed that our tent is up and running long before they've even chosen a prime site. What looks like home to one of us doesn't suit another. Mary Nan and J. Kent also spend ages looking for the high and private. Dick is quick, and Harold lags. Sometimes after pitching the tent, he changes his mind. Dave and Morgan don't bother setting up until after dinner. Two nights here, with a hike planned for tomorrow, will make a welcome break from paddling.

While we're eating dinner, the sun sneaks around the edges of clouds for the very first time, lighting slow fires over the land. I'm lapping up the warmth. The light is most delicate after 10:30 p.m. I stay up long after the others have zipped up for the night. I'm never sleepy under the midnight sun. There's another kind of rest to be found in translucence, and as the last traces of cloud float away, the glacier puts on a ball gown for me, eschewing the cold grey of day for bridal white and old ivory lace. A misty shawl lingers below the tops of the mountains. It's past midnight when I bow deeply and go to bed.

Summer Eden

A perfect day is when reality exceeds our dreams. I have to begin with the sun, its head thrown back spilling anthems from its golden throat at dawn, and when I divide the waters to squat and wash, I am speechless before its abundance.

Here are my actions,
a quick small poem.
I've got the hang of the trip,
the work, the people, my own pace;
the drill of pitching tents and paddling six hours a day.
I've whittled down my wardrobe to a uniform. A down sweater
doubles as a pillow at night and is the first thing I pop over my head when I wake.

Under the sky's proscenium, the Leidy Glacier is matin's event. With twenty thousand years of ice on the move, the Leidy's leading edge drops thirty floors, sheared raw by gravity and the knives of blue tides.

The glacier has become a metaphor now for the Arctic of my childhood imagination. Without any coherent picture in my mind at age ten, this mythic land – this archipelago of nineteen thousand islands in the polar north, was a place to get lost in, where a ship or a man could be swallowed up; a white-scape without words and weather all the time. The unrepentant snow falling on ice, falling on glaciers. All rising together now, we sing, *Oh Canada! Our home and native land! ... The True North Strong and Free! ...* Visceral, the northern frontier writ ragged on the Dominion of Canada's pink map.

"*Acá Nada*!" proclaimed the Spanish sailors in dismay when they visited the coast of Canada. "Here's nothing!" "Many Whales, No People," reported Baffin and Bylot after a failed attempt in 1616 to find the North West Passage. Then Dr. Frederick A. Cook's and Commander Robert Peary's rivalry turned the race to the North Pole into the media event of 1908, continuing the romance of *Arctic as frozen land of ice and snow.*

I said that the Leidy is the event, but that is not the only one. Let one of us move out of the wings of my peripheral vision onto centre stage, and no matter the distance, my eye will pick them out. A tent stands out on the tundra like butter on a bed of asparagus and our red kayaks look startling under blue sky.

The cliffs we're climbing today take a direct hit from the early sun and burn like a wall of flame. From sea level all of them look unclimbable, but Dave has a mountain goat's instinct for finding a route to the top.

We tune up our muscles with a gradual traverse along the shore, keeping the glacier in sight. Morgan, who is as keen a plantsman as I, dawdles among the wildflowers, digging into the flower book and comparing pictures with the *real McCoy*, memorizing names and counting. Fireweed licks rocky niches with crimson flames as we follow each other in single file, switch-backing between boulders and shelves too high to climb.

I like the honesty of rock. It's no-nonsense gravitas as I make giant steps, or reach for a handhold to hoist my torso on to the next ledge.

I look down and see things getting smaller. Hang-gliding in the air between boulders is my idea of flying, but when the scree starts to slide, watch out. I have to will myself not to reach into the side of the cliff for balance, lest the rubble break away under my wedged-in feet. My long legs are perfect for extra leverage and what I don't have in muscle I make up for in stretch. The air is the sweetest, cleanest air in the world and my lungs exhale a loud, "Yes!" My hat regulates body temperature so I can roll up my sleeves. From above, someone yells, "loose stone," and I listen for the hollow echo of rock teetering on rock, which tells me that it isn't going anywhere even if it is loose. We're winding our way into the clouds, and when we haul ourselves up the last vertical before lunch, Dave proclaims, "We've just climbed about 1440 feet at about 45 degrees ... and we did it in under an hour."

Now that we can study the glacier with a bird's-eye view, we're admiring the dark, moiré-like ribbons snaking vertically towards us on the surface. While the Leidy looks like it's sleeping now, we figure from our collective wisdom that, over millenia, the ice has been on the move, flowing into the widening valley, down to the sea, but not as one piece. Layers have surged at different speeds, forming crevasses that draw water deep within. We'd have to walk on it to listen for running water, but possibly a river is flowing underneath, and we guess that the decorative banding is gravel, silt and boulders which have been forced up out of its river tunnel.

We're sprawling in a windless nook of grass and smooth stone for lunch, when Dave decides to build a cairn to mark the summit. We list our names, countries and the date on a slip of paper and stuff it into a ziplock bag. It's the country bit that feels slightly heroic, planting our *flag* in the manner of the North Pole expeditions. At the rate materials break down in the cold, I can imagine a lengthy list as climbers add their names to it over the next hundred years. Or perhaps it'll be a disappointment to those who imagine themselves the first to gaze at the glacier from this height.

Leaving the glacier behind us, we strike out across the stony uplands looking for a different way to return to camp. We wind down a gully just following the lay of the land in the direction we want to go. Suddenly a creaky chorus exhaling, *Asssz! Aaaah! Prrrttt, prrrttt, prrrttt*, stops us in our tracks. It sounds like so many wind-up toys running out of steam. One by one, five dun-coloured stones rise up, batting frightened eyes in their ridiculously tiny heads, revealing snowy bellies on short, feathered legs. We've disturbed their siesta and, as one body, the Rock Ptarmigan lose no time in toddling away from this straggle of two-legged predators. Already these beleaguered birds have peregrine falcon, snowy owls and rough-legged hawks to worry about in the summertime, not to mention wolves and gyrfalcons in winter, but nature grows them a cold weather costume of snowy white feathers and fine feathery snowshoes on the soles of their feet. They can even dive from a height into a snowdrift, to hide their tracks.

If I had to compare the beauty of the bald-faced rock we climbed this morning with this Garden of Eden, I couldn't. We crest a ridge and look down now on a scooped-out valley, a vast catch-basin for the melting icecap. Myriad streams suck and trickle, then widen into shining pools that slither over the mile-deep steeps and planes to sea level.

At the end of the ice age when the climate warmed, dead plants decomposed into wet masses on the airless, soggy ground to form peat. That's the black sludge between the permafrost and tundra. We're descending now, over a well-developed hummock field of metre-high knolls, which look and feel like cushions. The Arctic Dryad, which is the territorial flower of the Northwest Territories, crowns these hummocks, nesting year round in their fluffy, dead leaves for insulation. Their little rose-like flower-faces, which follow the sun in summer, have succumbed now to showy seed-heads, in which the plumes topping the seeds have unfurled into feather-dusters. Purple Saxifrage, so loved by bumblebees, blooms around all the Dryad domes in the wet borders.

Tundra without rocks is worse than walking on a plowed field after a night of torrential rain. Luckily for us they're propping up the hummocks, bordering the streams and dotting the valley with stepping stones of all sizes. Even the occasional *erratic*, encrusted in eye-stopping orange, ebony, and lime-coloured lichen, adds punctuation to the miniature forest. On higher, dryer ground the springy carpets of the silver Wood Moss crunch under the thick soles of our boots. Emerald moss hugs the sodden banks of streams.

The only feature that mosses and lichens have in common is that they both lack roots. They simply shrivel up, sometimes for years, dormant until a source of water revives them. Instead of roots, mosses have delicate, hairy rhizoids, and lichens, rhizomes, which anchor them to the surface. While mosses can feed themselves by photosynthesis, lichens are more complex. E.C. Pielou writes that lichen is a fungus that grows its "vegetables" inside itself.

I love this landscape without trees. The tiniest breeze flutters the lemon petals of the Arctic Poppy and sends shivers through the fifteen-inch haloed heads of cotton grass. This is as tall as it gets. The only way to see it is to get down on your knees.

My downward path is pure free-fall as I zip around stunning clumps of Tufted Saxifrage, still blooming creamy cups. I change direction in midair so as not to squash them. I'm light-headed, skipping over a riot of mountain sorrel, Arctic Blueberry, lychnis, alpine chickweed, thrift armeria, purple heather, and tear-shaped wintergreen.

Winter is beginning to sprinkle reminders of itself like confetti between the greens. The prostrate Arctic Willow is one of the first plants to change, dotting the landscape now in electric apricot and yellow. What it lacks in summer bloom it makes up for in the hot lobes of its furry catkins, where transparent hairs absorb sun like greenhouse windows do. When I hold them in my hand I can feel the heat.

Morgan and I trail behind the others. He picks up an ochre-coloured puff mushroom from the ground and squeezes it. A mustard cloud of a billion spores sails away like a rumour of new life.

Pulaarpunga – I Pay You a Visit

The campsite is still in shadow as I wriggle out of the tent at 5:30 a.m. I dream about mornings like this when I'm in the city, hoofing it away from the group to take the measure of the land, alone. I pan the view in a circle, noticing that the mountain ridge on the far side of the fjord looks close enough to touch. I imagine tracing its countenance with my finger as I would a lover's face, dissolving the distance between us with tenderness. But my itchy feet want to climb, and now my breath is coming hard. Once or maybe twice, it seems, the tundra tosses me out of its springy arms into the flaming air and I fly up and over the top of the miniature forest. I lap up the land, memorizing its lines and textures, tracing them with my eye over and over again. It's a fool's game to try to hang on to every nuance, but I want more than broad brush-strokes. Sweeping vistas, after all, are just the outline of the landscape's complexity. "The land," writes Barry Lopez in *Arctic Dreams*, "is deeper and more subtle than we can know."

At this hour I am tuned to perfect pitch. In the immutable space some lucidity in the air strums a note: a simple song on the tongue of growing things – music and me inside it, drawn beyond any geography I know. I'm caught up in the loop of the life and death of ice, the quick shift of seasons, and the precocity of birds. What keen breath is this that fans these flames in my heart, then leaves as quickly? Suddenly the strumming ebbs and I fall out of the sky into the concrete distractions of solid ground, into the plop and shuffle of rotten ice, and the arpeggio'd splashdown of the red-legged guillemot.

Now the diamond hardness of light blasts up the flanks of rock-cliffs like footlights cranked to high, inscribing each fissure and fold in shadow-black. From this bright eyrie, the scope of this stage far surpasses my ability to overlook it. I take it in on held breath, alert to the possibility that something is about to happen. I think that waiting in this way is attention of the highest order. It allows things to come forward, to show themselves.

I thought retracing our route to the open water of the Inglefield Fjord would be humdrum, but the Arctic is full of surprises. For the first time we get to paddle up close to ice. The sun pries it off the ends of glaciers, adding perky partners for the aging bergs already waltzing in slow time up the fjord. They sail along the shore nudged by the invisible current and often run aground. It's odd to see these freestanding sculptures orphaned on the rocks at low tide.

i t b e g i n s w i t h a w a v e • a lone hunter paddles home
we take it as invitation his arm scooping us in for a pot of tea

by the time we've beached he's sitting on a rock
white sealskin boots/pants   legs crossed/smoking a curved *pujut* (pipe)
his family   sparkling/shy
under lowered eyes

seems the polite thing to do
when you enter someone's home (or hunting camp)
to greet the host *sainanq*

can hardly tell male from female us
lining up hilarious in long underwear
baggy-kneed (so glad mine's form-fitting/legs long)
hair all but invisible under toques wooly hats baseball caps

I would sit with him puffing his *pujut* like my father
be called out for noticing
still running on city current I hold out my hand
grip his soft paw and tumble headlong
into the mountains and valleys of his hand
fingers light
framing my slighter topography
his eyes see through me to something more distant
the habit of silence in his body perhaps awakens
in me a just hurt
could I prolong my *pulgar* (visit)
unlearn restlessness
take Zen Master Ummon's advice
When you sit just sit?
but my sure-fool resists I seek talk photos
plop myself beside him on the rock
my words breaking glass
Inuktitut's backwash feathering air
yet stitched up blind I can't leave it alone
corral his wife's eyes
re-enact my journey *avani* (north) arms tilting wings
back out on the fjord the ghost of home holds my hand
pulse quieted now by
flesh blood bone

Soo thank you Inudluara Inudluara Goodbye goodbye

After lunch with the Inuit at Nunatarssuaq, we enter the open water of the fjord again, rounding Kingingneq Peninsula's bulbous nose, before crossing to a campsite on the east end of Qeqertat Island for the night.

The horizon wavers.
Inside the sweet interference of precious light
tall ice rises quietly out of the fields of glass.
Here the mountain lies down beside sky,
your kayak intersecting the sea-plains
in the translucent flush of late afternoon.
Strained by too much beauty,
reason wants to lose its way:
this benediction in the timeless moment
making explicit the world without shadow;
here the promise we had hoped for
replenishing the soul's gape;
here the pattern, a reminder of the whole
we can't quite grasp
and through the desolation
a return to the work that grows the heart.

Light is becoming a major theme and the incidental music of my days. I'm swimming in sensation and mad with the beauty of it.

Fear in the Face of It

We're paddling strongly, seeing it coming, taking it head on. If rocks could float, I'd believe that a white bouldered sky had laid itself down on the water, filling in all the black spaces. An ice-jam of *growlers* – ice less than one metre high – stretches ahead of us for miles, as far as I can tell, from the front seat of the kayak. Dave calls it *brash ice* and he tells me to keep my paddling rhythm steady, even when the big chunks lift us half out of the water and we slither sideways. We carom bow-first into the packed ice, crashing from one swirling lump to another with crabbed strokes. My abdomen tightens with the effort of a right-hand thrust, skids off the hard surface and sets the ice bobbing. Too late for a good stroke, I reach with my left arm and dig into mush. Our passage sets the rubble-junk spinning and submarining before it closes in behind us. My adrenalin's up and I'm having fun. Doubts about my endurance flicker through my mind but muscle power routs my thoughts and steadies me. I ask Dave how he knows where to head next. "Mostly intuition I guess," he answers as he steers us away from a dirty bergy bit, listing and about to roll. His paddle connects suddenly, and as we surge ahead he adds, "If we can get into the lee of that island the ice'll get better." The island's a long way off but I trust his considered calm. Dave doesn't ruffle easily. Like soldiers moving forward on the front lines, we vanquish the next chunk of ice and the next, elated when we escape into polynyas, ice-free pools, where upwelling currents of relative warmth prevent the ice from freezing. We burst into one now, drifting under a leaden sky waiting for the others to catch up. I stare into the pool's impenetrable black eye. Not even the sun pierces its closed heart.

It would be nice to dally here in the sudden tranquility but Dave permits only one quick photo. We press on, whacking a path through the unhinged sea. Today's brash ice shattered yesterday's hall of mirrors – an exotic beauty that makes me forget the terror which lies just underneath the killing edge today. It's no stretch for me when I stare into the unforgiving depths, to imagine Neqivik's revenge.

After the imprisoning ice we lapse into silence and an easy sea. I'm struck again by the quick light. The puppeteer who holds the clouds on the ends of his fingers calls the shots, the mood and the pace. Today the stage was set for tragedy, calling for a closed sky, cool strength and a palette of grays. As never before I felt the iron will and the fragility of ice as we slashed our way through it, its broken edges ready to break us had we been in lighter craft. But tragedy loses its edge if it lasts too long, and slowly, slowly, the puppeteer spreads his thumb and forefinger parting the clouds for the exuberant sun. We turn up our faces now for that first hot kiss, and grinning at what we've accomplished, unbend our bodies and look up as if we had just shaken free of a dark dream.

The rhythmic chunking of paddling makes me dozy now, my mind gone to mush. I hum to myself a small song, and for a while it's enough just to hold the unwavering light behind half-closed eyes. Nekivik's warning turns to trance, as I dream of scaling the shiny backs of the biggest bergs and wheeling into the deep solitude of sea and sky.

Then I hear music
                    the music   always here
under the roof of the world
it plays only for me   and I   inside
its body   surrender to the weight of its bow
            wet inflections   summoning
old clichés of water slurping under summer docks
                        waves in Mediterranean caves
I'll never forget at low tide

                                    I   a seal
slip into turquoise depths   give ear to the undersea
    but this is before I open my eyes
                                wanting to know
the source of sizzle and rivering   to see
    how the water converses with ice
        how exactly the sun and wind wield their sharp knives

There   running down the wind-polished cheeks of ice
the sun's hot finger pits the steely slopes
            dimples into a million melting lips   erupting
the young streams leap for their lives into water
                        the way cliff birds   toss   chicks
out of the nest   to flounder and swim

            the Arctic carousel's tinny tunes take on more muscle
as fountains gush from icebergs over cantilevered rims
drilling holes
            in the sea-round with their hard sound

There's trouble   the water is arguing with the shifty ice
    but with the grace of tall ships icebergs accept it all as their due

they are cousin to water
    before mingling their fresh melt with salinity
they know themselves to be the primordial frieze of glaciers
    waiting for weather to inscribe

Once beyond the iceberg's baritone reach, the timbre shifts. The uncoupling of winter's slow compression sings with a different voice now. Tiny animate prisms release bubbles and crinkle the air in the highest register of ice-music.

Ice it seems, is
a glass animal cavorting around the bow.
In a frenzy to be born
whimsical creatures
candle the light
and capsize
with tiny sighs.

I am a listening ear, attuned to each solo and recitative, the anecdotal dotted notes ornamenting the unwritten score. For surely I'm learning to read what is unwritten. No one calls the tune, the key or the time signature that I can tell, but then why do I even think this music has been written for me: that to unravel its mysteries key by key is even important? And this is the point – right here in the middle of the symphony, in the counterpoint of ice-music I'm waging a battle between surrendering to that music and recreating it in words. The loudest voice claims my ear, one sound at a time, and the chronicler in me who wants to bring it all home in writing is labeling, comparing: killing the wild energy around me. As I loop along the curved line of these thoughts, the words of Rilke come to mind. "... we keep longing for a foothold." How to let go my foothold – yes even of language – and slip, unminded, into the 'polyphonic thrum'.

I'm captive now as the tumultuous rhythms tug at me with the insistence of Sunday bells. The pulse of something bigger than my own pins me and upturns the words jockeying for position in the pitch and tumble of my mind. A plodder, a simile hound, that's what I am. That the rush of water sounds like violins is partly true, yet similes or even *thinking* for that matter, only jam another wavelength trying to grab hold of me by the scruff of the neck. When I finally let the slur of words go that are trying to attach themselves to each pitch and glissando, everything re-arranges itself. I breathe. Every voice and timbre shines with the clarity of a perfectly fingered fugue. Desires vanish, save the urge to follow the trajectory of this meditation in an effortless connect – a meditation that shapes me whole, brimmed up and not wanting.

Not only have we been paddling for hours, but if meditation is a constant curve, I've been following that trajectory with a rare single-mindedness. We haven't arrived at the campsite yet, although it looms like a brown smudge beside the glacier in the unreadable miles ahead.

The grand score begins to gather up all the musical threads woven in my ear thus far, when – and this is what I've been waiting for – the conductor, if there is one, adds a grand finale to take me home.

An intense pressure has been gradually building below the threshold of my ruminations. The hammer-stroking of big runoff is turning the air blue. It comes from deep inside a city-block of ice as if it contained within its core an inland sea awash with tides. A torrent is ripping through its weakest arteries, rupturing in an unstoppable hemorrhage: a time bomb's slow violence wrapped in waterfalls.

Now give this waterfall to the string section in this afternoon's orchestra and let them saw untiringly against the iceberg's crescendo.

Icebergs speak with the authority of a single voice hurled through space. My arm stalls in mid-air, paddle forgotten. Thunder like gunshot obliterates mind and words when a shudder runs along the spine of this great mother ship of ice. Her flank fractures free and she begins to roll from side to side ponderously like a reluctant world, the sky teeming ice. Waves rush away from her sides unraveling the calm sea; arrive under us, lifting and dropping the kayaks as they pass on through. I ride the crest of the cadenza and like every other living thing I recognize without words the echo of the primal voice.

The silence that I come north for is an illusion after all. There is no such thing as silence. It just pretends to be thin as air, permeable as shadow. It tries to tuck its head under folded wings to fool us but still its heart beats. Silence is weighty and intimate, and out of its all-encompassing womb it births the music.

Ruminations & Rewards • "I feel fear in the face of it," says Dave, while we prepare supper. "It's too big for us. Too far beyond what we know and feel comfortable with."

I've volunteered to make the salad and balance a cutting board between rock and slope, while I pare the bruises out of the apples Dave has been repacking in the front hatch of our kayak for too many days now.

"After today I've gotten a new respect for ice. I never dreamed I could paddle through something like that."

"I knew you could do it Rosemary," he kids. And then, "We travel in our own bubble of equipment. Don't have to worry where our next meal's coming from. We're heavy, and the Inuit light. They're connected to the land, we're seeking it, travel here for that reason. But all our *stuff* prevents it. It's deceptive." Morgan scoots forward on his bottom and begins to slice up the cabbage.

"You know sometimes I really believe that I *get* what I'm seeing. But our time here, it's such a small slice," I moan, "just a few weeks in summer." I'm discouraged, knowing that I'll never really belong in the north.

"You'll have to come back in the winter." Morgan teases. I make a face at him and shiver.

"We need a new relationship with the land," Dave continues. "We compartmentalize it, separate it into cities, countryside, wilderness. Needs to change ..."

"We split ourselves when we divide up the land," Morgan interjects, removing the seeds from the red pepper and slicing it into the cabbage.

"Yes, but we have to divide it. It's the only way we can handle our stuff, the population. Ownership, for instance." Then, "Ice brings up questions about my relationship to stuff – proportion, death, what's beautiful, you name it. I guess I feel safer with a little order."

"I wonder if we're being hypocritical?" Dave muses. "We take it for granted that we can buy the latest thing but we ask the Inuit to stay the same. If they want to hunt from motorboats instead of kayaks like they do in Canada, why shouldn't they? We love to visit their traditional camps and watch them keep the connection for us. There's the argument that we should only use stoves not fires, but then no one thinks where the fuel comes from either – Inuit too ..."

"We can ignore that 'cause we don't see the impact it has on the earth," says Morgan.

"... What we need is to have fires but feel the impact directly. Connectedness is living with the consequences of our actions," says Dave.

"We bury our garbage and then think we've solved the problem. Allows us to over-consume and to disconnect." I nod and we agree we'd all become activists if we had to live with the direct effect of our over-consumption.

I guess the guides thought we'd earned our stripes in the brash ice this afternoon because after wolfing down chili, coleslaw and cornbread, Dave tells us to settle and close our eyes. J. Kent quickly pops into

Mary Nan's lap and she yips in glee only to discover it's just her husband. He snuggles in while Dave takes us on an imaginary journey to the Scottish Highlands, tickling our curiosity with hints of peat, smoky flavours and heather. When we open our eyes he's holding a bottle of Glenmorangle, 18-Year-Old Scotch whisky. "Ooooh," we chorus and hold out our mugs. Dipping my nose in its oaky depths I sigh. While we lollygag on the rocks making our two fingers last as long as possible, J. Kent announces that he feels a poetry fit coming on and wants to recite. He stands up leafing through his mental library of Robert Service and launches into

This is the law of the Yukon, and ever she makes it plain:
"Send not your foolish and feeble; send me your strong and your sane –

"Wild and wide are my borders, stern as death is my sway;
From my ruthless throne I have ruled alone for a million years and a day;
Hugging my mighty treasure, waiting for man to come,
Till he swept like a turbid torrent, and after him swept – the scum."

J. Kent gallops on, six rollicking beats to the line. Then we beg for more. Even though the whiskey's honey warms my throat, the lines of the poem raise the hairs on the back of my neck. I picture winter storms that rage for days over the ice-bound sea; hundred mile-an-hour winds that blow sleds and dogs away, never to be seen again; the killing cold and the weight of silence. The Yukon that Service describes is not so different from Greenland, although there are neither rivers nor gold here, but what he did know about first-hand was the epic and the elegiac.

I made the acquaintance of these alliterative twins
the first time I set foot in the Arctic.
Standing inside their circle,
I knew myself to be half finished.

What lies beneath knowing who I am –
to get to a right place and that not done yet?
Fear of too much beauty or not enough –
wanting to know how to die   forgive
to love for heaven's sake.
Hungry for home.

I venture into the silence where there are no voices to tell me who I should become. It is the ground and text of an unfinished poem to which I am adding my own personal canto. I'm stunned by the epic grandeur surrounding me. It is too heavenly. I'm turned inside out, air bound, consorting with angels. The epic has become the filter for all my reflections: the elegiac, the mood. Time *present* feels like no time at all: its joyous imperatives suspended in a meditation on *now*.

I need details to keep me anchored. In this mood I've been fixing on real things: gathering facts, visual impressions, and history. Animals, for instance, their mystery, secrecy and humour. I'm the first to see the dark curve of the narwhal's back break the surface or the whiskered faces of harp seals playing hide-and-seek with our kayaks. Earlier today, walking alone on the tundra, my eye freeze-framed the flight of an Arctic Hare. It stood on tiptoes inspecting me, black-tipped ears arrowed up, then jack-knifed snowy-white and free up the tabled rocks and out of sight. This runner at rest stopped me in my tracks, the air crackling between us. I waited, locked in the embrace of his concentration. How I longed for ten ears to catch the thumping of his heart, his silent footfall – to get that close to the earth. In the quickness of our intimacy, I saw myself another animal. I became *part* of what I was looking at, and it was looking back at me.

The fleeting glimpse of the niveous hare captured me before I could try to appropriate it or make it tangible (to memorialize it with a camera for instance). My desire to possess overturned by what Carl Jung calls the *moment of arrest* – the exchange with the hare, a slippage, a homecoming. The epic and the elegiac intertwined.

I turn to the idea of geologic time and my picayune place in it – another kind of letting go – and know it to be the opposite of seeking fame, even of leaving a headstone. Building the cairn above the Leidy Glacier made me wonder if I wanted even that much of myself remaining for the land to remember. If I remove myself from the equation, retracting my need for permanent memorials and boasting, abolishing front-of-the-line obsessions or any desire for my name to appear on a donor's list, will I suffer loss or find my soul?

Time Is a Passing Animal

We hike miles back on the land and spend the better part of the day stalking a small herd of Peary caribou grazing in a meadow. The first to see one whispers the news, and instinctively we drop to our stomachs, binoculars glued to our eyes. We count eleven drifting across our vision, in pale relief against the high dark cliffs blocking the cloudless sky. The soft breeze accentuates the deep silence and sets the pom-poms of cotton grass bobbing as the meadow grasses roll in waves, first hiding, then revealing the herd foraging the rich pasture. In the seamless continuity of time and light there are no sudden moves in this scene. "Time here, like light, is a passing animal," writes Barry Lopez.

Their loose pairings suddenly disperse, and we track two, which lope up the valley and disappear over the top. We give chase and an hour later spot them grazing behind a screen of rocks. Dave creeps forward, then waves us to follow. When he flags us down, we duck.

The female lifts her head and looks our way with watchful, deep eyes. About the size of a large deer and delicately coloured, her smoky face and legs blend into oyster tones that spread like cream over her rump and belly. Her antlers are the size of a moose's rack and look too heavy for her slender neck to bear.

Rangifer tarandus pearyi belong to the deer family Cervidae and have been around for about 120,000 years. Named by Robert Peary, of

North Pole fame, they are smaller and lighter than mainland caribou, and remind me in size, if not colouring, of reindeer. They do not migrate, but live in scattered herds in the Canadian Arctic archipelago and northwestern Greenland, fattening up for winter in terrain such as we are hiking in today.

Males reach sexual maturity in one year and females will birth one calf per year, beginning at two years of age. The calves, a marvel of nature, are capable of running ninety minutes after birth. Thus, they can keep up with a moving herd.

After a catastrophic die-off in the 1970's, the Peary caribou made a healthy return for two decades, but are now again on the endangered list. In the winter they *crater* or scrape away the snow's surface with their big crescent-shaped hooves to reach the lichens and mosses they count on for sustenance, but global warming is causing early freeze and thaw, which lays down ice over the vegetation. They either starve outright, or use up valuable energy pawing for food, which makes them vulnerable to attack, as wolves are lighter and can travel on snow crust that caribou would sink through.

In Greenland, an aerial survey showed a healthy population of 100,000 in the 1960's, cascading to the dismal count of 7,000 – 9,000 at the present time. We agree between us not to reveal this sighting to the inhabitants of Qaanaaq when we return. Over-hunting is another reason for their decline.

Hiking back to camp, I practise covering ground like an animal. I don't want to break the conversation I've had with the land today.

I'm sitting up in my sleeping bag to catch the last honeyed rays of the sun as it rivers through the open door of the tent. It's 11:45 p.m. Lazy puffs of air dome and then drop the glowing walls, snapping softly.

I'm unminded, drowning in the warmth. This must be how a lazy fly feels basking inside the tiny furnace of the summer poppy's golden cup.

Tonight I have 20/20 vision. Shapes look equidistant in the dust-free air. Like the lens of a field camera, my eye skips through the foreground and clears the middle, reaching infinity as if foreshortening did not exist and the periphery did not fall off into a blur. I begin an experiment at my feet, panning through nutty green mats of heather and the backlit leaves of alpine fescue, to where shadows creep inside the hips of boulders, their boundaried bulk outlining the shore. Deep blue underscores the middling shores of ice, and then, smooth as silk, the sea humps its back and drapes the mountains around its shoulders. Near and far, reflections of icebergs, double. They read to me as fine print on the glossy pages of the sea.

So much of the mystery in the Arctic has to do with seeing, or its winter opposite, blindness. Inuit live two separate lives. In summer, light drenches the mind. I can see who I am, when my black double climbs with me up the rock heights two feet from my face, or flies, arms outstretched for balance, over sloping ground.

Surely winter's permanent night is a mystery: a time of discovery rather than seeing, when hidden faces from memory, dreams and unconscious stirrings arrive unbidden. I suspect there's more to read here than meets the eye. I asked Hans in Qaanaaq if he likes the dark months, and his face softened as if he was seeing at this very moment the moon and stars illuminating the ice. Fond memories are always full of the waxing moments, but what happens when the moon is hidden, and one is left deprived and groping? "Summer weather is boring," he tells me softly.

We couldn't find a name on the map for this campsite and at supper I decided to call it *Boulder Slopes*.

The Absence of a Script

What I like about adventure travel is the absence of a script. The closest we come to one is to roll out the area map once a day and take our bearings. Ice covers ninety percent of Greenland, pushing people all the way to its sparse edges, which is where we make our camps. Situating ourselves on the map each day is a good thing to do: the only way I can keep my bearings is this daily reckoning of distance travelled.

Our destinations are always provisional and inexact. Dave spreads the map of Inglefield Fjord on the ground and we look on over his shoulder. NORTH 77 degrees, it says. Boulder Slopes' green shore lies sandwiched between massive glaciers, which drift off the map into the white expanse of the icecap, marked IKKE OMÅLT, or UNEXPLORED. He traces a line north-west with his finger, showing us the channel we might sneak through, if there's enough open water between Josephine Peary Island and the floating tongue of the Tracy Glacier on the north shore.

This almost inaccessible wedge of rock riding high above the sea was so named by Josephine's explorer husband, Robert Edwin Peary, making hers the only woman's name on the map of the fjord. A beautiful, "refined" woman voyaging in the "dreaded realm of the Frost King," she gave birth in a hut in 1893 as winter was setting in, to a daughter, Marie, on the Bowdoin Glacier where we are going to camp.

From dancing school in Washington, where she first met Peary, to the gun-toting hunter with her Winchester lever action rifle and Colt revolver, she was the first woman to take part in an Arctic expedition: her motive for going north possibly strengthened by a wish to get rid of her mother-in-law, who not only lived with them, but accompanied them on their honeymoon.

Her husband Robert was always obsessed with being the first man to reach the North Pole. He tells his mother, "Remember, Mother, I must have fame and cannot reconcile myself to years of commonplace drudgery." A career navy man who understood how to cultivate the establishment, he created the Peary Arctic Club, made up of wealthy and influential Americans who would provide the backing and applause for his many dubious claims of discovery.

He was a man who forced you to take sides. In tackling the *Big Nail*, as the North Pole was called, he was arrogant and ruthless, treating resources, people and animals as pawns. Four hundred dogs, two white men and at least eight Eskimos died in his service. "The great tormentor" was one Eskimo's description of him. In New York, he was a hero.

Peary's mania for personal glory led him to make mapping errors, naming islands and channels that did not exist. He claimed to be the first man to set eyes on Axel Heiberg Island, though it seems he couldn't possibly have been in position to have sighted it; and that the northern end of Greenland was a huge island separated by a channel, both of which he named after himself. He mistook a mirage off Axel Heiberg for a great land he named Crocker Land, proven false by Vilhjalmur Stefansson's exploration of the Arctic archipelago in 1914.

Of course it is tempting to discredit Peary after the records have been examined. At the time, he was a blazing star, and could not be proven right or wrong. It was when he was lecturing in New York on the formidable hazards of reaching the North Pole that Dr. Frederick Cook, who once served as surgeon on two of Peary's expeditions, was already on his way. He had set out with only two Eskimo companions, and in the words of Knud Rassmussen, "I was able to verify that it would be hard to conceive of a more intelligently equipped expedition than his."

Cook's philosophy was the polar opposite of Peary's big business approach. He did not believe in struggling against the forces of nature, but instead, in seizing the opportunity, if it should present itself. Small wonder that when he announced that he had reached the Pole a year before Peary, a vicious slander campaign to discredit Cook erupted. Poor Peary was apoplectic and his financiers in the Peary Arctic Club outraged.

It is not known if either explorer really reached the Pole, as neither man brought back *scientific* proof of their presence there. As one Berlin astronomer, investigating Peary's claim, said, "None of Peary's methods are dependable. Even if he had reached the Pole he would not have known it."

I muse about Josephine as we go. She quite sensibly dressed in skins against the winter temperatures, but often topped her fur suit off with a long dress, New York style. Because Marie was the first white child to be born in the north the Eskimos dubbed her the 'Snow Baby'. In her first winter in Greenland, when Robert was off exploring, Josephine wrote *My Arctic Journal* in which she describes her distaste for the domestic squalor associated with family life in an iglu. She strikes me as being two kinds of Cinderella, a spirited adventurer and one who bridged two worlds, clothed in her own unique version of an Arctic ball gown.

Yesterday's brash ice has drifted north overnight, bobbing in harmless ice pans in front of the campsite. We slide easily through them on our way out, but nearer to Josephine's rock they get chunkier and we hit them hard. Now that I know how tough the kayaks are, it's like a game. "Like bumper cars on the midway at the Toronto Ex, when we were kids," says Dave.

And like a kid, I sing a campfire song I've known all my life.

"Land of the silver birch / home of the beaver / where once the mighty moose wanders at will / blue lakes and rocky shores / I will return once more / boom-buddy-om-boom-boom-buddy-om-bum-boom-boom-buddy-om-bum-boom."

The rhythm is perfect for paddling. Then I sing everything else I know.

As we close in on the Tracy Glacier, the katabatic wind sweeps down its spine, blackening the water and whipping our faces with its stinging tail. With a sudden drop in temperature all desire to look for a passage departs. When we see it, it's dammed up with skyscraping ice. We turn our back on the glacier and take the longer route down the south side of the Josephine Peary Island. Soon we'll complete the circuit of the Inglefield Fjord and rejoin the main body of water which we crossed by motorboat six days ago, then proceed west to Qaanaaq along the north shore.

In the nick of time Josephine's island provides us with a narrow pull-out. Our bladders are bursting. What bliss after three hours to strip off our survival suits, pee, eat and then spread-eagle on the hot rocks for a snooze in the extravagant sun. But with the mainland to reach and a camp to find for the night, we can't dawdle. We leave our sleepy niche in the ledge and paddle away for the oldest movie in town, playing now across the face of the sheer cliffs. Feldspar, quartz and mica in black, aubergine and green ribbons ripple and twist in an old agony of heat. The story of metamorphic rock coming up cool and forever mosaic –

Fifty million years ago, and mysterious as atlas headings
(Eras of the Earth, Continents Adrift, Worlds Beyond)
these preposterous cliffs took their first step
and, raised up
by earth's great wheel-driver cracking its antic whip,
were fashioned here – my neck craned now
to the deranged crenellations of rock carving sky.
And balanced on ledges, the nests
of the winged raptures
lifting and turning
in a feather-blizzard above our kayaks.
As if some golden hand cupping sky
had captured loft and glide, for light to pen-stroke
a blueprint vane, shaft and barb.
Trust the guillemot, ancient
butterfly of the sea
to tumble out of the sky like laughter.
In black suits,
they dive, red legs dropped
to skid. Settle.
Their folded wings logo a lopsided moon
and the mystery
of where winter's moon goes in moonless summer
becomes clear to me.

Once more in open sea the steady pull of paddling reels in my thoughts. The air feels cooler on my face as we cross the line between sunlit and black water, and my spirit sags at the sight of the cold and unwelcoming east-facing shore-cliffs ahead drowning in shadow. They stand between the sun and ourselves and I see no tundra there. No welcome mat. The map, silent. We paddle in silent dismay until the guides agree on *something* that looks inaccessible to us. "Where are we going to pitch our tents?" we wail. Morgan leaps out of his kayak while we wait and scouts it out. He jumps from one ledge to the next, disappearing into a tundra gorge – yes, there is a slice of tundra – about a 45 degree drop off on the far side of a gully. I crane my neck to follow him. When he reaches the *troisième étage* the multiple chins of ledge hide all but the top of his head. He shouts that there's a lake up here and lots of room for tents. There's a powerful creek and that means fresh water. We take it.

En Plein Air

By turns the tent feels like home, or when nights are fine, just another set of walls to escape from. Housekeeping is a cinch. Mesh pockets circle the walls so I can reach for anything from a lying position. I've assigned the one by the door for film; the next for hats, eyeshade and sea sponge in its own waterproof bag. Long johns and bed socks overflow the third, and the one nearest my head takes whatever doesn't find its way inside my fleece jacket, which, stuffed and zipped, becomes a lumpy pillow. To hand is my ditty bag and journal. *Simplify, simplify,* warned Thoreau, and I have taken pride in my Spartan approach. Witness the neckerchief cum hanky and the ghastly green cloth, the size of a tea towel, which is never wet or dry but doesn't smell, suspended from a clothesline over my head. Sunglasses swing on closed arms from a loop on the ceiling. And this is just my side of the tent.

My dream of sleeping under the sky – the stars and moon are absent in summer, north of sixty degrees – came true last night. Morgan has slept out twice and suggested I do the same. I jumped at the idea, spreading my sleeping bag on a ledge that was fifteen feet wide with a sharp drop to the fjord. A wall rose to the next level above, at my back. Al and Shawna's tent was about twenty feet away, and J. Kent and Mary Nan pitched theirs just above me on a higher ledge. I was glad to learn the next morning that J. Kent didn't take his usual midnight pee over the edge.

Humans are infinitely more adaptable than animals. That's both true and not true. Here's what I mean –

Caribou and muskox snooze
standing up
bears recline in a grassy hollow or den
ground squirrels lemmings spoon & curl
subterraneously
humans can & do slumber anywhere anytime
sitting
lying
occasionally standing though not for long –
but sleeping
under sky
that's special

Summers in Algonquin Park, I learned about sky. I remember we'd cut balsam boughs and feather the sharpened branches into the ground for a fragrant mattress. Blazing stars offered up galactic worlds and drew us dreaming into the sweeping arc of the Milky Way. We'd wake at dawn in the purling mist soaked in dew and tell how many shooting stars we'd seen.

On account of our being two-legged vertebrates, our visual *take* on things is mostly top to bottom. Once at Esalon in Big Sur, California, I stood on my head observing the right-side-up people as they padded about on the grass, but, come to think of it, I never did spend much time looking at the world sideways. Stretched out on my new ledge-bed, I confirmed an earlier discovery that Dave and I made.

We tried the sideways thing at the Leidy Glacier and saw how, in a slant world, names lose their meaning. A name, after all, can tell us something about form and function, so we don't mistake an iceberg for a cloud or a castle, in spite of shapely similarity. Viewed side-on, an iceberg, as object, needs reinterpreting. The twin image becomes a Haida totem, a stone edifice taken corner-on with gargoyles, or Ghibelline turrets topping stone walls in opaline and pewter.

The horizontal prospect is usually left for children to discover, or, if you desert your tent for one fine Arctic night, *en plein air*.

I can't say how much I slept last night. The idea of closing my eyes seemed such a waste of time. I kept peeping. Although others were tenting around me, I had not felt so exposed before. I knew I was the only one awake, and so was as alone as I had wished to be, walking the shore before supper on the first night at Nutak.

I lay for a long while thinking about the Inuit, who must have used this ledge as a sleeping platform. I thought I heard laughter coming from their invisible tents and was comforted by this. The wall at my back seemed alive with power to protect as I gazed at the mountains, across the fjord, burning in the dying fire of the sun. Behind the mirth a white wind thickened the air and I recognized the glacier's voice, and then that other one – the licking sea, the gulping, licking sea, and the glacier's howling ... and the creek ...

... the light, lavender now, and the brightness gone from the tops of icebergs: the mountains' glow behind them dowsed by night; shadowed ice, somnambulant, abstract almost, between the slate sea and the formless sky. On the edge of sleep again, it seemed that the life of ice is not unlike our own – much of it a lonely passage. We grow big, bigger, and under strain relinquish parts of ourselves whose loss always feels like a death. We do "… melt, / Thaw and resolve (ourselves) in a dew," I muse. It seemed at this late hour to be a good thing – a drop of dew …

I said that ours was an east-facing campsite, and so I wake early, sweating in the full sun. It's 6:00 a.m. I unzip my bag and stretch, checking the position of last night's icebergs. The world is intact, the set pieces in place and the sky as blue as it should be. I scale the jigsaw cliffs with lazy eyes, and imagine spidering up their tilted ledges, so solid it's hard to believe the surface of the earth is always turning beneath us. I have that fact on higher authority but need none to declare that the unarguable rock is flying its true colours right now.

Picture autumn putting all its crayons into one basket and coming up RED. That's close, but the gilded light won't leave the cliffs alone. It burnishes up the slants and bevels of rock's fixity and clothes the coast in gold. This could be Arizona, New Mexico, The Tablelands in Newfoundland, or the desert cliffs east of the Black Sea. Not Greenland. And as if this palette isn't rich enough, on every level a yellow tent.

Time to get up. I pick my way down the boulder bank to the creek, wash and then laze, nude on a rock in the sun. I creep past Al and Shawna's tent, greedy to have as much morning as I can before the others stir, and wedge myself against the wall to write.

Accidents and Exploration • A soaker isn't fun. Nor is a sliced hand – cut deeply along the heel of the palm and pressed into the paddle grip with every stroke.

Before pushing off for the day, the guides leave the kayaks to the bow paddler to hang on to, while they help the others into their cockpits. Our job, Gail's and mine, is to prevent the kayaks from floating away. My foot rests on the bow, wedging it in place between the rocks. I see how the tide is sucking at the shore and that Gail is daydreaming. "Don't be bossy, it's her boat," I tell myself, seeing it coming. "Just shut up."

Suddenly her kayak parts company with the rocks, and by the time I've shouted, "Gail get your kayak!" it's too late and I've gone in after it. Ice water pours into the top of my right boot and sliding on a greasy rock I sit down with a splash. Morgan has me on my feet in a jiffy and holds me up while I dump out the briny mess, wringing out the liner in my boot and my sodden sock. I'm mad at Gail – this being the last in a list of co-operative tasks that seem to have escaped her notice for the entire trip – like the dishes and pegging down the tent, quibbling about enough air, at night. The tent sweats if there isn't enough air, and besides, while we keep our bodies clean, we can't wash our clothes, and Gail's socks stink.

Now the drama is over, I take my place in the bow. Dave gets in and, reaching for something on the deck, swears quietly and gets out again. He motions to Morgan, who grabs the first aid box, and they spend the next ten minutes stemming the flow of blood from Dave's wound. Morgan cleans and binds it, their backs to the group, so no one else guesses what's going on. Without a word they get back in their kayaks and we're off.

I'm impressed with the quiet dispatch with which the two of them pulled off the repair. Dave's palm needs stitches. In its friction against the paddle grip it bleeds through the bandage. He tells me he cut it on the broken whisky bottle stowed in a paper bag under the bungee cord on deck. He's been meaning to dump it overboard for a week.

The story goes back to our second cold evening. We're sitting on the ground around the *kitchen*, following the agitated path of a bottle of Scotch that Harold is waving in the air as he delivers the first of many such excited monologues. Oh my god, he loses his grip and it flies out of his hand and splinters on the rocks. We send up an anguished cry; the guys falling to their knees in a mock attempt to lick the rocks clean. Dave picks up every last piece of glass and puts the bag on the deck of our kayak for disposal. Harold apologizes sheepishly and we forgive him – almost.

In spite of my wet foot I am full of peace today, content to paddle at less than a walking pace. I can see it in the others too, as each paddle-pair moves with the synchrony of unconscious habit. We travel in a loose group with the exception of Harold and Dick. Harold's pace conforms to his animated conversations. He forgets to steer, doubling the distance he has to paddle. Suddenly, like an errant star, he shoots across our bows, stops paddling and starts off on a new tangent when we catch up. Dick never says how he feels about this, but he's such a steady tripper I'm not sure he notices.

The kayaks have become an extension of our bodies after all the uses we have put them to. They serve as freighters, icebreakers, cruise ships – everything except hunting craft. For all their bulk, they navigate the water with great delicacy while promising stability. I'm brim-full with the thrill of propelling myself by my own muscle power; refreshed by the dip, dip of synchronized paddling, at a tempo that permits reflection.

Take ice for instance. All the events in the life of an iceberg fall under my eagle eye now as we glide past the latest show. Bergs are top-heavy because their underwater parts melt first. When they roll or shatter, gravity's winch wrestles old slopes into sharp inclines and heaves underwater ledges out of the sea, tall enough to buttress sky. The racket steals the air out of my lungs until the seas' cold calculation settles the ice-colossus into new equilibrium. Thus, by counting the diagonal water lines along a berg's flank, I can tell how many times it has rolled.

Waves and currents begin to undercut a new shoreline now and with time, perforate into dripping caves with filigreed arches. What was once submerged comes up smooth, still wearing its ice-skirts of turquoise tulle. The dialogue between the ice and me is uncomplicated. Like a good poet, the ice doesn't *tell*, it *shows* its range of expression in every line and texture of its ephemeral life.

Lunch is over and we're threading our way through a stunning armada to Quinissut, a hunter's camp next to the Hubbard Glacier. I have no eyes for the cliffs today, only ice, and of course, ears for the music – the evocative music. All the time that I've been wrapped up in – yes, even participating in – the symphony of sound, the amorphous shapes of icebergs have been evoking in me serial and fantastic pictures.

Nothing under the sky has a human face.
Not from the tiniest ice-clones winkling
around our kayaks to the middle distance and beyond,

where the old growth ice-giants march
in slow procession across the arc of the sea.
They watch our passage with sightless eyes –
wild, beautiful and alien: nothing I've seen before.

Wilting spires frame turquoise arches full of sky. Pure gothic,
we say, imagining the soaring light in great cathedrals.
A Roman ice-encampment tables along-side a titan

sheered midway to its mantle-core;
its flat, triangular face inked in purple shadow.
Prophets fly out of alabaster delivering urgent messages,

their foreheads glistening,
or are they perhaps the starving hunters begging
Nekivik to release the sea mammals?

Clearly, we can't help ourselves. The ice sets our imaginations ticking, spinning stories, which need words to complete them. It's as if we must edit the magic, drape it with adjectives in order to ground it in our clay-poor brains. Whimsy rescues us from the inaccessible and strange.

It's just as well that Quinissut, our home for the night, is flat. My overstretched imagination can do with a rest. While my eyes hitched a ride on the ice this afternoon, the cliffs halved their grandeur, descending now as meadows unfolding in graduated slopes. Over decades, the gravity of their slide accumulated earth-mass, oozing over the melting permafrost to land in lumpy grass banks at the edge of moraine. After "The Little Ice Age" (roughly 1450-1900), the toe of the glacier pressing down on this place retreated, leaving inside the rim a mile-wide dry bay of silt, sand and clay.

A lonely hut breaks the monotony in the middle, advertising this as another traditional Inuit hunting camp. We land our kayaks where the moraine and tundra meet and make our kitchen at the grassy border.

In Search of Fresh Water • First things first, as we used to say in my family when faced with something unpleasant to do. The wet boot liner is sticky and cold and that won't change unless I find some fresh water. Dave tells me that, over *there*, and he points in the direction of a high ridge on the far side of the moraine, he remembers a freshwater stream from last year's trip.

I change to hiking boots and with one *wellie* under my arm, set off over the clattering stones on the beach. The closer I get to the hut, the higher the stench. Rotten narwhal heads lying in the sand, more skeleton than flesh now, are beautiful in the gruesomeness of sightless death. Skin, taut over bone, barely conceals the congealed blood underneath: shines metallic, like a dragonfly's wing. Abandoned in loose coils, the slack inner tubes of gut await decay. Rotting is a slow process in a cold climate.

I carry on toward the ridge, lined up at a right angle to the shore. So far, there's no fresh water and I hike past it and come to a fertile corridor on its far side. A beautiful valley graduating upward to the sky is flanked by high and unstable walls. As I begin to climb, the campsite disappears and suddenly I am out of sight and sound of another living soul. No predators to worry about either. Polar bears don't come this far south, I'm told.

When I was twenty-two years old, I climbed the hills of Loch Lomond. Dozens of sheep paths lacing the gorse gave me the idea that it would be fun to try and tackle a sheep. That's when I discovered how fast they could run. The only thing to tackle here is the slope, which, like the Highlands, tantalizes you with the promise of a summit, only to level and lure you on again.

I see evidence now of a streambed. The silted crease of the valley is undulating downward with token wetness glistening in the light. I'm happy loping up this pocket of Eden, and even if I don't find fresh water I'm loving the surprise of willow and wildflowers. Perhaps last year a sparkling stream did course from some meltwater lake above, banking the soil and feeding the diminutive forest under my feet.

The ground gets mushier and levels off. I find what I am looking for. A tea-coloured pool, fringed with grass, wears a collar of ice. I douse boot, liner and sock in the fresh water and wring them out. In the second it takes to stand up, I become aware of the stillness inside my valley. If I listen now, I can catch a slight riffle in the air beyond the walls on my left. So I scramble up the sandy slope wondering idly what could possibly be on the other side, but before my head comes level with the top, I feel it. A sensation of void, of falling away, a chasm in the pit of my stomach and something about a subtle change in the sky takes hold of me, all at the same time. Fingers of cold slide over my face and I know.

Why should I be surprised that at the foot of the scree and gravel wall below me, ice begins its slow march out to the fjord, a mile across to the next moraine, then swings its great fist upward into the face of the icecap? To take it in in a glance, I must scan the Hubbard Glacier from left to right. I look down on the impossible surface, studying the jagged peaks and dark wanderings of its crazy fissures. I make a quick estimate of the steep bank. While it sprouts grasses, there's no handhold and it's really nothing more than a sand dune. Even if I could slide down, I'd never get back up.

Funny, how we always want to climb to the top when we're at the bottom of a thing, and how the reverse is also true. It's enough to be making this solo exploration, and I turn from the riddled glacier, top dressed in dirty snow, and hike, my clean boot and I, back to camp for a late dinner.

Short Cut to God

My wet sock and boot liner froze overnight, and so incidentally did I. Bagged up in my warmest clothes, I hugged myself against the chilling ground-breeze rolling down the slope over my body as if it were flowing water. I wonder now, if I had dug beneath my mattress, how soon I would have come to ice. You never can tell how deep the permafrost is. Once on a rafting trip in the Yukon, I was wakened every night about three in the morning, when the aching cold would rise through the stones on the gravel banks where we slept.

In two weeks the temperature will dip enough to begin freeze-up. Because fresh water freezes at 0° C and sea water at -2° C, one of the first signs of winter, or *ukioq*, will be the random scrawl of free-floating ice crystals, called frazil ice, filming the surface at the outflow of fresh-water creeks and around the shores of melting icebergs. As seawater cools, it absorbs more brine, and when it's on the verge of freezing, it sinks, leaving an inch on top of fresh water ready to freeze all at once into an oily 'soup'.

Inuit call ice *siku*. The naming of every age and stage begins with patchy frazil ice, or *puttaq*. As it cools, it turns to slushy grease ice. This thickens, then darkens, appearing almost as transparent as water. Its elastic form bends over the swells, now called nilas ice, and will support the weight of a bird. About four inches thick, nilas changes to gray ice or young ice, also called first year ice, when it becomes opaque.

By spring, first year ice may be four to six feet thick. If summer doesn't melt it, it becomes second year ice, blue-tinted and hard. After a couple of years, the ice thickens to ten or twelve feet. Anything older than two years is called multiyear ice or pack ice. Then there's fast ice, snow-ice, shore-fast ice, pancake ice, needle ice, candle ice, and the permanent polar pack or paleocrystic ice, which forms in the open polar sea and can be fifty feet thick.

Last night at Quinissut, Harold and I talked long into the lovely night, standing on an elevated bank above the fjord. Neither of us could possibly go to bed. Between ourselves and the sun-licked coast in the distance, icebergs and their poorer relatives rubber-stamped their exact shapes on the glassy water. It seemed as if each set piece sat on an identical plinth, coupled by lavender hues and cobalt, safekeeping the sanctuary of deepest shadow, hidden. We mingled our voices with the silence, for silence was the voice of ice last night, and we three held a mighty discourse on the source of things. "... break the wineglass, / and fall toward the glassblower's breath," writes Rumi. We did, and when we had said enough, it was well past midnight and we went to sleep: Harold to his tent and I to my bed of saxifrage under open sky.

For last night was my second night to sleep out under sky. Taking up no space at all, I spread my sleeping bag on the hilly-sided tundra and crawled in, just like that. I felt like a pilgrim, a vagabond or an explorer.

> I lay back and gazed at the sky circling the land, circling me –
> the world as it has always been, and I, lying in its flowery cradle.

Now I lay me down to sleep
I pray the angels my soul to keep,
if I may die before I wake,
I pray the angels my soul to take.

I have been inhabiting an impeccable world tonight: the light unmasked everything. All evening the still air has been worshipping the ice – this white water landscape – so heavy with melting. Does ice get closer to its essence I wonder, as it yields inch by millennium inch to some cold silence beyond itself?

That the saxifrage blooming around my bed-for-a-night is already spirit, seems true to me – its long-lasting flowers, a kind of declarative innocence.

  For it is innocence, isn't it?
The moment before green speaks its name
  or declares its intentions;
before form decides to be itself
  or its own reflection.
It's when my whole body laughs.
I pray that the alchemical winds
  will love me more than I deserve,
each breeze a new pipe dream for tomorrow.
  I own the thought
that I am longing for a shortcut to God.

Monday Morning • and we're paddling to our final campsite today, but I'm not mentioning our return to Qaanaaq. I'm never the first member of a group to break the spell and begin the unravelling of family, which we have become over twelve days. As long as we're moving, I'm hooked and present. Today's prospect, as we head into the widening mouth of the Inglefield Fjord, is new. The last big berg in the kingdom of ice cracks and rolls with a gush and a sigh, tic-tocs in ponderous obedience to sudden truncation. Ice spews skyward, seaward, shredding water as it heels. In the commotion, the air holds court with a slow return to silence as we're lifted and lowered in its lively wake.

Crags now turn to bluffs, becoming escarpment, as we pass the towering keep of Castle Cliff on our way to the abandoned settlement of Kangerdluarssuk. Most of earth's slow history is contained in these Precambrian rocks, which form the core of the continent. All day, light and shadow have been retooling their textures.

Not a trace of wind riffles the narrow waters of the Bowdoin Fjord as our kayaks skim still water. The red mountains spill a darker version of their sun-drenched contours onto the perfect surface. We slip inside its curves, travelling blue sky, and in the centre, a glistening back surfaces and dives. "Narwhal," I whisper to Dave. He misses it, looking up instead at the mesa-like summit to our left. "Tomorrow we'll find a way up there."

The odiferous remnants of the hunt greet us at the landing, and at the top of the bank above the beach, there are two wooden buildings and a rack with a kayak, which indicates this site has been used recently. This is no idyllic cottage setting, no weekend getaway; instead it is the lean-to-will-do philosophy, which is responsible for the bare and broken plywood patching the frame of the sleeping cabin door. A plank serves as a bench outside, and folding chairs have been left where they were last sat upon. I take a peek inside the smaller building and wonder what wild impulse compelled a hunter to riddle the painted bureau with bullets.

Lucky for us the camp is as generous as the one last night. There's ample meadow climbing up the mountain to spread out on.

In 1970 an American military transport, bringing school children from the area to the Kangerlussuaq Airbase further south, crashed on this mountain and a cairn erected here in their site bears the loneliness of all such places: grief put to rest in a stone's inscription, then walking elsewhere.

Did the mountain tremble when the plane full of children fell out of the heavens into its frozen shoulder I wonder? Did earth heave and buckle before returning to the unbearable silence? If nature has an organizing principle, knows where it is going, does it also have a memory?

Once I came to an isolated beach and was moved to tears by the miniature profusion of fern and flower quivering in their boggy islands, halfway up a rock ledge above my head. In the keen wind, I bowed before them, using words like faithful, patient, precious to describe their beauty – that there should be so much beauty and no one but myself to see it. I felt a longing for something beyond possession and the memory of it: to be more than a witness of this lush laboratory of cell division and death. But the joke is that my lavish respect neither ruffles their petals nor encourages them to any excess of their own. "Beauty ... offers us its own existence," writes Simone Weil in *Waiting on God*, as the mountain behind our camp does this very night. Keeping my eye on it won't change a thing.

And so, what else is there to do but witness the disequilibrium of ice, the rotating seasons? Who can make sense of such waste: the random death of youngsters cut down by weather or machines? What difference, the cause now? Our lives are uncertain. We long for what we can't articulate.

Whether it's the shadow spilling down the mountain now or the land holding grief in its bones (a comforting thought), I feel the desolation of the place. After the tragedy, there were intentions to build a community, but the project has been abandoned. Unused building supplies lie forgotten on the ground, although students still come with their teachers to practice hunting skills.

Each of us is preoccupied with our own thoughts on this last night and we take our strolls alone.

A solitary figure hunkers on a rock,
rigour of farewells tomorrow.
Memory already scratching the future
wants to arrest this light-kissed dance
tell of last rays
leafing gold on roof-pitched gullies
of night's mute
unscrolling, tundra's pitch to tide's ebb –
whose silk sigh is our balm.

So much has happened in the windless kingdom.
Purple, lingering at the heart of it, sums up the heedless days.

Sydegletscher Walk

So far I've loved them all. That antimatter of rock, cold air and water we call glaciers. Progeny of ice ages, cumulative snowfall became rivers of ice, sifting its timeless syllables over sloping terrain, and everywhere its unknowable weight bows the earth.

I've doted on the petrified face of the Heilprin Glacier from the top of a grassy dune; adored the dress-up charms of the Leidy's mouré skirts stitched with glacial till from the high point of our luncheon cairn; and from the sea's vantage, I've paddled at a respectful distance from the Tracy Glacier's grim seawall, wide as a continent in spite of the polar paw bashing it to bits.

Even so, I'm not fooled by a glacier's apparent stasis. I look up at the frozen river-fall floating its fat tongue for the tides to lick, and will it to make some grand gesture for me. Why me? Because I'm here and captive in time's fleecy mitt, ready to bear witness to the planet's antics. I beg of the glacier a little chaos, a small truth, some whinnying momentum perhaps, which might disturb the serenity of this Arctic house. I am prepared for the mess of evolution.

But there are some facts that apply to the Arctic's slow unfolding, which I am so impatient to witness. Most of Greenland lies beneath an ice cap covering eighty-one percent of the island, and at its thickest is 14,000 feet. If I could fly to the top, I'd see a polar desert, mostly uncharted, stretching 680 miles wide and 1570 miles north to south.

Underneath its great mass, much like the unexplored recesses of the human brain, are buried plateaus and concealed landscapes. Deepest in the centre, the icecap slopes, then flows into the sea from every direction. The tail-ends of these slopes are the valley glaciers blowing katabatic winds in my face whose night speech sounds like ululation.

Inside a glacier is a furnace. On the basement floor of ice next to bedrock, heat from the earth's interior thaws the snow crystals that are always re-grouping and changing shape under pressure from above. Equilibrium, struggling against the forces that would make it fly apart, is overcome, and this outflow glacier begins to move.

A glacier either flows or retreats some inches to many feet in a day – more now with warming temperatures – and begins to look like a house coming apart on different floors. While the roof is more or less solidly fixed, the floors or ice layers separate and slide over each other (the upper ones more quickly than the lower) and in response to gravity's persuasion, garner a free ride to sea as icebergs.

At the same time, water seeps into the cracks of the rock below. Subsequent freeze and expansion completes the separation of rock from rock and the newly jacked boulder-bits begin a convoluted journey inside the glacier's grip.

Take a ride in a Cuban *cococab* over potholes, and after the sagging seat with no springs has done in your spine, imagine the back wheel flying off into the oncoming traffic. Retrieved with a slam and a kick, the wheel now wobbles on, but the chassis feels like it's been fractured and may leave you discarded like excess baggage at the side of the road. You might call the side of the road the moraine and yourself the clay, silt, sand or an erratic stand-alone at the edge of the party. The glacier's chassis, fracturing as it slides over the uneven bedrock, could land you in a crevasse or an underground river, but, without a doubt, in a few thousand years, a cold swim in the sea awaits your rock scourings frozen into mansions of ice.

Meanwhile the glacier has clawed out a landscape between

mountains, filling the valley from horn to outwash plain with rock rubbish, meltwater lakes, cirques and crevasses.

This morning we attempt to climb the ridge Dave spotted yesterday afternoon when we were paddling into the Bowdoin Fjord. He leads the way up, but his feet are losing their grip and are raining stones and gravel on our heads. We're backtracking now along the shore and terminal moraine in the direction of the Sydgletscher Glacier.

From below, the surface of the glacier looks puffy as a duvet, crevasses having already self-destructed in this mid-sized ice field. A giant step up, and I see that the snow is corn snow, granulated and easy to scrape away with a boot.

The sound of rushing water gets louder now and a fast creek is bully-washing the glacier mid-slope, sucking silt, stones and anything else in its path, in a tear to the sea. Rocky outcrops, which resemble miniature *nunataks*, poke through the snow surface. Pools, like so many glass eyes, have formed in the depressions, but the water's clarity makes a mockery of depth. Each ice-crystal reflects the sun's dazzle. Ice slivers float like peaceful islands.

I'm shouting into my tape recorder, taping now the sharpish *schrunnch* of snow under my feet, and finding only adjectives to describe the love affair my lungs are having with the air. Lungs big as a whale's are breathing me. Stepping-stones, spaced conveniently in the torrent's frantic mumbo-jumbo, make an easy bridge, and now on the other side, I notice a shrinking snowfield in the high moraine.

"When we stepped from the moraine into the snow, did you notice how wet the stones were? The ice is melting from underneath," Dave offers.

"I'm guessing this glacier – the one we're standing on – is in retreat," I say.

"Yup. Ten feet a year."

"So ten thousand years ago, everything was under ice." I circle the air with my hand. He nods.

"See those lines along the cliffs, where the colour changes? That's how far the ice went, and then, moving under pressure of its own weight and the pull of gravity, it flowed everywhere, gouging out a depression in this river valley, and others, and the ocean flooded in, creating the fjord."

"Was there more fresh water then – glacier fresh that is – than there is right now in the sea with all the melting?"

"Hard to say. It didn't necessarily melt all at once," he answers. "Melting always reduces salinity. Even now the salinity of this water is much lower than say, the Queen Charlottes', and there, it's a lot lower than in the Sea of Cortez, which is like the Dead Sea."

"Huh?"

"Two reasons. There's a lower rate of evaporation here, so it melts more slowly, and two, we've lots of fresh water coming off the icecap. In winter there's hardly any evaporation – just a little bit of sublimation."

"Sublimation?"

"That's when ice evaporates gradually without going through a liquid stage."

"Like dry ice." Dave nods. "So," grasping for the little I know, "this is all sedimentary rock now. The stuff over here that looks more solid, is it still ..."

"Yup. We're still looking at sedimentary rock but with different mineral content, producing different colours. That green rock we were breaking apart at lunch – that's a good example of how soft rock can get."

"Why is there sedimentary rock here and gneiss over there?"

"Gneiss is rock which has been metamorphosed. It may have been sedimentary rock earlier in its life and then it was exposed to extreme heat and pressure – so, for whatever reason, that rock was exposed to more heat than this. It's older, and may well have started out its life much further below the surface, before tectonic activity and erosion exposed it."

"So gneiss is more compacted, eh? – all those patterns weaving through it."

"You can see how it's compressed and folded. It's hard to imagine, 'cause we think of rock as being solid. We know that ice moves, flows, bends – so does rock."

Morgan picks up an oval stone and passes it to me. I notice that the blush of its roughish surface is deeper than the colour of my skin. In the centre of one side is a pink circle, a half-inch in diameter. Two brown bands surround the eye and are separated by a pale thin ring. Decaying plant material must have sandwiched its indelible mark between this and another stone bearing the mirror image. The weathered pigments are soft, like other hieroglyphs I have seen. Not exactly an eye, but nature's idea of one.

I always bring back treasures from trips. The windowsill in my studio at home is awash with shells and bones from lagoons, flushing coves and beaches –

winkles abandoned on the beach
abandoned on my sill
I touch the empty house of bone
recall my toes cold
sand losing heat to encroaching night
– a grainy song of leavings
the sun's rays crossing over
home out of the question
as tide's out-take lays
a slat fence across wobbled dunes
Chesterton Beach
exactly nine-thirty
sundown a fact

Also –

I've silver dollars from Cortez,
an *Astria Giberosa* from Sabina,
who claimed it would bring me back to the island;
I've coral, barnacled stones and turbans from the Queen Charlotte's
in the pearlescent bowl of a blue clamshell.
North beach, Quadra Island.
A Japanese glass fishing float washed up on Moresby,
beside the vertebrae of a seal.
The porous parts in the hills and valleys of its endoskeleton,
filigreed with tiny holes –
a bone-scape, reminding how sun honeycombs ice on a glacier.
Ageless nut-sized knot of driftwood
extends its twiggy arms like a wishbone's nerve –
hard as polished stone.

And this is who I have become.
Part curator, part dreamer,
I hum to the tide's tune, palming stones.
Pants, bulging, threaten to leave waist for ankles.

The shiny pools and the rash creek are burning up in the hot sun. The creek knows it, of course, as it buckets along yodeling goodbyes; and what's to come I feel now as a shiver under the skin of the sun-tempered air. I was not thinking of one thing becoming another when I stood in the trip's "magic middle" a few days ago, but even light-all-the-time moves the days forward. My inclinations, if they are not to evaporate into thin air like dry ice, require embodying now.

I get down on my knees and begin to photograph the bubbles trapped in the lacy ice-collars hugging the rims of pools. I get lost in this and it's only later, after I discover I have forgotten to put film in my camera, that I realize I don't really care. Suddenly I'm on the brink of a new idea. Something I've been thinking about needs clarification.

It's a given that I want to return home with a story. Photographs have always been a major component of that story, but now they seem to me little better than field notes. I love form and light, but what moves me is the tension I feel between the life and death of the seasons, the counterpoint between stillness and movement, the blurred edge of light and time. The way silence invites a conversation about music. What the camera leaves out is what I so passionately want to remember.

Pictures isolate the subject: then frame it. They fix time. I worry that, at the pool's edge, I've stolen just one ice-crystal to try and explain a glacier, and that what remains is a fragment, neither story nor history.

"We have the experience, but miss the meaning," writes T. S. Eliot, and I am afraid of losing that. I needed to see, without props, the Arctic Hare stretch itself tall to get a good look at me. Had I been fiddling with f-stops, my eye would not have looked into its eye. To have lost that moment of breath-held intimacy would have broken my heart: memory and intimacy intertwined – making story.

What if I put down my cameras? How can I keep track then, of the overload when the tide is always coming in? Photographs at least keep events straight, yet my need for order is at war with wanting to be alive. Now. I write a journal but relish the loss of time, days and dates. We go to bed late, sleep in, pack and paddle at night, eat anytime. Our biological clocks recharge under the abundant light, and days elide. If I could just trust that inside that vertigo is the story: the one that feels bigger than my puny life; the place without walls; the power locus of memory and sensation. And a place of meditation.

I want it. I am afraid of it.

And so a glacier calves. I grab my camera. Today, close-ups of ice-crystals take my fancy. I like to get in close: catch the shine on wintergreen leaves, the mushroom spores Morgan released after our hike, streaming away into another dimension. I have to weigh my burgeoning desire against the pleasure I feel when my camera becomes an extension of my right arm. That speaks of another kind of intimacy. I would miss it.

Notwithstanding, I am getting closer to choosing the "coherent narrative," over a fragmented record of photographs. Muddle has its own circular logic. It requires sitting. Integration comes after the flood.

Already Going Back

When does the going back begin, I wonder? I catch a whiff of it when someone voices out loud his thoughts about the charter we're going to catch in a few days, or Wednesday's forecast. I know then, they're already moving away into time and to another place I don't belong. I feel a wrench, and for just a moment, chide myself for having swallowed the illusion that our lives are now deeply connected and we owe some lasting loyalty to each other. Who are these new chums, who have chosen this polar world to travel in? Do we even know ourselves?

Glorious it is when wandering time is come, says the Eskimo song. In these words I recognize the longing to leave the familiar and be off once again: to turn the momentum, which has been building for months within, into more than a dream. For one who has fallen under the Arctic's luminous spell, it means a continuation of the journey into self, with the land as mediator. I love training my powers of observation, which the naming of things kindles, and how that first step lodges *place* more firmly in my heart and mind. With past memory providing substance for ongoing inquiry, muscle and sinew remember and renew the landscape's claims, implanting its geography in my feet.

When I take the land's measure, I take my own. On the way to Nutak on the first day, I asked myself if I was up to it, meaning more than the required level of fitness. I'm speaking now of courage, the pluck to imagine myself in this immensity: to align myself with whatever is in store and take the consequences, glad there's no escape.

Yet I wonder if, in the dream of going north, we don't all imagine a bolder, more heroic side to ourselves popping out, like a rabbit from a hat, to take us by surprise; some secret character we've yearned to express sneaking out from the wings to take an experimental spin in the midnight sun: giving ourselves some wiggle-free room to let down our hair.

Does J. Kent picture himself as a man of mettle "staggering blind through the storm-whirl" as, rising to his feet, he recites *This is the Law of the Yukon?* It's not every night that I play the comic heroine by falling into the cooking pot. After many calls to dinner and still dozy, I stagger out of the tent and, skidding down the slope, land in the spaghetti pot. A clown is born as we all get the giggles, and when at dessert I start drawing the pot and the runaway noodles with my spoon in the chocolate pudding, Dave wants to know how come I've lost it.

At last I see Gail smile from the far edge of the group and I imagine that for her, the icebergs are mere extras on the Arctic's outsized stage. I picture her suspended in the gods at the top of a ladder in the Metropolitan Opera House painting the finishing touches on Rigoletto's forest. Is she more bound to the story of a father's loss, perhaps, than cooking up a new one about ice's "strip-tease?" ("Seen one, seen them all," she told me once, referring to icebergs.)

Was I already going home when I slipped the stone Morgan gave me into my pocket? Or just now, when the fair-weather part of me is noticing that our window of sun is two-thirds shut and likely to close altogether? No longer the euphoria of the fifth day, when I thought I could go on like this forever, but a feeling of blue-for-farewell settling under the surface – and meanwhile, we are striking our tents for the last time and packing out every trace. Wind flattens the choppy water and clouds spit drops.

No reflective bowl of mountains coddles us on our paddle out of the Bowdoin Fjord. A backward glance reveals the Sydgletscher highlands as *materia*: rock's backbone more nuanced now, without contrasting shadows. The opposite side of the fjord is softening like a charcoal drawing, the sharp outline of undulating coast smudged in with a thumb. Icebergs pose in front of the horizon like crumpled paper, as sky's Quaker grey ceiling opens and closes according to the will of the upper winds, which, releasing occasional stingy rays of thin yellow, footlight the vertical ascent of the shore cliffs to our right. Not a chance to land for miles.

Of course we are used to long stretches of paddling, and I regret that while I am fitter and wishing for another day, I will soon stow my paddle and haul the kayak out of the water. For ours is the final trip of the season, and after landing in Qaanaaq, we'll strip the kayaks, sponge them out, secure the rudders, then carry them to their cradles in the paddle house for winter. Spray skirts, life preservers, pogies, unclipped paddles, seat casings, hatch covers, kitchen utensils all need to be sorted and stored. Our survival suits will fly back to Canmore, Alberta, where two months' brine and sweat will be washed out for another season. But first, Dave and Morgan will peg them to the line outside Han's hotel to dry: dummies all, their yellow arms and legs pedalling in the breeze.

We see it now from a long way off. Qaanaaq, with its painted houses backed by the icecap creaming the edges of the mountain behind the town, looks deserted. An archeological site, nearly one thousand years old, Qaanaaq was just another coastal slope where "yellow and green grasses grew." Its peaty soil had been enriched for centuries by the blood and oil spilled from the whale and narwhal that were hunted in Inglefield's waters. Thus it was little more than a seasonal camp until, in 1953, the Eskimos living in the town of Dundas sixty miles south were moved there against their will by the Danish Government, to make room for the American Air Base, *Pituffik*, at what is now called Thule.

Jean Malaurie describes the 1953 American invasion as "The Iron Age" in *The Kings of Thule*. What had once been a peaceful valley of virgin tundra was turned overnight into a city of "hangers and tents of sheet metal and aluminum." Eskimos nearby told of the sky filled with planes for days, of yellow smoke and diesel smell carried on the wind; the sound of the "panting:" of machinery turning silence into pandemonium. Trucks, cranes, bulldozers and caterpillars worked on and on, walling off the bay so it would be immune to the tides, building networks of straight roads in its nine mile length. This place was to serve as the Strategic Air Command's new atomic base in the north.

The airbase's heart thumps now, but I can't hear it, or smell it for that matter. As we draw near Qaanaaq's shore, Dave starts howling. One by one the wavering sounds of wolf-like cries join in a harmony of howls as each tethered dog raises its snout to the sky in an eerie welcome.

Ow, ow, owhoo-oo-oo! Ow, ow, owhoo-oo-oo!

The pebble beach grates under the bow and our kayak comes to a halt with a lurch. I step out into a foot of water and grab the bow toggle. We help lift each kayak up onto the beach, setting them down in a row. Without words we begin clean up, our back and forthing rattling the stones under our boots.

Later • Berthe has prepared a special meal for our final dinner tonight, and after our exuberance has driven any other guests out of the dining room, the stories begin to fly. Ten of us, beaming after hot showers, have just consumed nine bottles of wine. No one wants to call it a night. Dave suggests we go around the table recalling special moments of the trip. Fixing on details again, I remember the narwhal misting across the fjord as they swam toward the hunters' harpoons, the prolixity of flowers and glistening streams in the Garden of Eden hike, and Harold's silly lateral progressions by kayak; others recall the feeling of suspended time, the miles carpeted with brash ice, the sea birds and the rhythm of our days.

More facts come tumbling out. Mary Nan now tells us that she and J. Kent have four adopted, grown kids. We're all amazed. How come they didn't share that earlier, I wonder. Anyone could tell watching them paddle together that they were a real team.

Dick, who has been reticent for the duration of the trip, hits his stride and tells us how he once hiked the Amazon, "Hiked!" we roar. "How do'ya hike the Amazon?" On weekends he plies the airspace over Chicago in his own hot air balloon. He even keeps a dog team, which he transports to Resolute Bay for a spin in December. Once he sledded to the North Pole. We laugh in disbelief and move on to a bottle of Port. And now, as we learn more of the private side of his nefarious pursuits, I dub him the quintessential American bachelor. When coffee follows, I turn in.

Unwinding

Now that it's time,
  the Twin Otter bounces
down the gravel strip on fat tundra tires,
  backs up, switches off. All hands.
Freight belly, filling up.

Ice buckled up in the bay
  spells out the tall grey sky,
wind's whinge and gull cry
  lettering the air last, before
the boarding.
  Ice's watch is done for us.

The trip is over but not the travelling. We're flying over Ellesmere to Resolute Bay at 18,000 feet in a cargo plane, and I forgot how cold they are. On the fjord I'd plan for the day ahead, because if I didn't, I'd be down on my hands and knees fishing kitchen supplies out of the hatch to get at a warm jacket, or suffer the cold for hours to come. Small mistakes carry big consequences in the North and I'm suspicious that some southern conspiracy is teasing me with the idea of home, where there's always a warm building to duck into when the weather is inclement. There, rescue is instant, excuses acceptable. As I smile at my myth-making, I'm reminded that this is just a modern twist of the ancient Eskimo belief that blunders might interfere with the natural order of things.

Dave sees me shivering and whips out his sleeping bag and tucks us in. J. Kent recites one more round of Robert Service over the engine drone, and in three hours we're back at Ozzie's in Resolute Bay for the night.

That's not the only thing happening. The other group from Ellesmere Island has arrived too and we're swapping stories in the dining room, our voices – mine too – deafening, as when the silence, after the music ends, is shattered by applause.

After the serenity of our days, time has whacked me on the back and I'm coughing up the imperatives of tickets, timetables, and alarm clocks. Where did I put my watch? What makes it manageable is that we're all in it together, experiencing the strange reversal of the steps we had to take to get here. The problem for me is that it's unwinding too fast.

One-room airports in the North always remind me of a party in full swing. If I could decorate the hum in the air in Resolute Bay's airport, I'd blow up balloons and fly them from the roof. I hide behind my group and spy on the locals. When the women catch me, and they always do, they smile. Eight Inuit girls standing in a circle gossip and giggle like the teenagers they are. None looks more than sixteen years old and each has a sleeping baby in the embroidered *amaut* on her back and a face as sweet as any Renaissance Madonna.

Against the wall, a little boy tilts his head up to rub noses with his mother. His peaked cap worn backwards slips off. She picks it up and pats it back in place. Big booted men in anoraks or plaid shirts slap each other on the shoulder and clasp hands, and a woman I scarcely remember from the day I flew in comes over and asks me about my trip to Greenland. Everyone is waiting, it seems, for something wonderful to happen: the whole town gathered to welcome the incoming plane. Workers from Iqualuit further south and miners from the uranium mine in Nanisivik on Baffin Island's northwest coast are returning home to Resolute.

Our flight is called and we board, bound via Nanisivik for Ottawa. Our route will take us southwest over a corner of Somerset Island, Prince Regent Inlet, and the barren wastes of the Brodeur Peninsula.

I'm sitting between Dick, my American hero, and a hydro man from Yellowknife who has been working on contract for three weeks in the North. The first lap to Nanisivik takes an hour and soon we're circling over the mountains to land on a high plateau. Rows of overlapping peaks are wrapped in moody blue veils of light under a cumulus-loaded sky. The road winds from the airport like a grey ribbon down the boney spine of the mountain to the invisible town below.

We have an hour, and Dave and I hoof it down the road, greedy for our last sight of raw beauty, sucking in the magnificent northern air before we're sealed into the aeroplane for good. I gulp it down as if it was the last drop of water.

When we return to the terminal for boarding, the heat from the packed room hits me full in the face. I snake through the happy crowd to greet the pilot who flew us to Qaanaaq two weeks ago. "Have you retired yet?" I yell at him over the din, and, as if this was a cocktail party, I steam away to find the next person I recognize. I'll talk to anyone.

The hydro man is standing in the corner with some other men. In fact, ninety-nine percent of the passengers are male. I slip in and find myself beside a barrel-chested guy who's so tall that I have to look up at him.

"Where'ya from?" he booms.

"Toronto."

He chortles, says, "I'm from Richmond Hill. My name's Butch. I'm a carpenter in the mines."

"Carpenter? Didn't know mines needed carpenters."

"Yeah. We keep the roof over their heads."

We log on to that instant shorthand which locates, assigns and looks for commonality and so often finds it. Butch turns to the hydro man, about fiftyish I'd say and balding, and they learn PDQ or pretty darn quick, that they were both born in Manitoba. Same town, same school as it turns out. Questions begin to somersault. "Do you remember ... ?"

"How's he doing ... ?"

"What street did you live on?"

"Yeah? What number?

"Thirty-two?"

"Did Isabel Duggan live next door?"

"Yup, nice lady. Know her?"

"She's the mother of the woman I live with," says the hydro man.

Bingo! The numbers match and we've all come up winners. Two Inuit guys overhearing the conversation from their perch on the windowsill break into broad grins and we all hoot and holler.

This very Canadian scene is right up my alley. Chance meetings in a land so sparsely populated always make for common ground. Everyone has a story of adventure or hardship to tell and it still feels like there are frontiers to conquer. Friendliness is a given. Besides, with the long distances to travel, there's still the love of a good yarn.

When I'm away from the North, I dream of the light. It's my way of coming up for air after the close-toned, drab days of winter. It might be light pouring golden libations over the high meadows at midnight, or a palette of pastels tinting the rarefied air. Whichever it is that I recall, I am soothed and can't wait to return. Neither has the light disappointed this time. I am bewitched and thinking about spirits; light's disproportionate presence tantalizing my mind. Air's dust-free clarity makes far seem near. I can touch the top of the mountain or walk ten miles in a minute, while at the same time the diaphanous space stretches the meaning of infinity.

That icebergs remind me of 12th and 13th century European cathedrals, for their soaring architecture is inevitable. Like shrines, they dropped the multitudes to their knees in awe before the Gates of Heaven which the arched ceilings and spires seemed to reach. Clearstory and rose window, by the way they captured light, brought home the connection between God and humans. The Arctic returns me to the age of mystics.

I remember imagining I heard the ancestors laughing in their invisible tents the first night I slept outside with the cliff at my back. We have all kept a sharp eye on *Sila*, "the great dangerous and divine spirit that lives somewhere 'up in the air', out in the universe, between sky and sea, hovering over earth," which we read as weather's mood. As the narwhals approached the foot of the glacier, I wondered about their souls.

Rasmussen recorded the belief that if an animal was not killed with respect, its spirit would return to afflict the *Nuna*, earth. It is within the living memory of some, that animals and humans could exchange places and communicate, that every element in nature had a soul. Great hospitality was given to captured animals. A little water would be placed in the mouth of a dead seal so that it would not go thirsty in the next life, and I question how these beliefs play out in the modern hunter's mind.

For days now, I've been unsettled by the hunt we watched at Nutak. There is no doubt which team those Inuit left behind on the shore were on. They hoped for a kill. But me? In that moment, I was afraid to root for anyone, torn over witnessing an authentic hunt to the bloody finish. But it's not the blood, I realize now: it's acknowledging the beauty of it that frightens me; worried that I would be less humane if I allowed it. I might construe the whale's death as the animal offering itself to be killed, the way Inuit used to do; believe that narwhals indeed have souls. I was guarding myself against the hunt's exotic appeal.

I recall an infatuation with bullfighting in my twenties. I lived in Seville, Spain and went to the *corrida* every week in the summer. The sunny afternoons were filled with fleet shadows in the golden sand, of crimson capotes, the flash of the *muleta* at the final *estoque*, the touch of death and of black bulls. If the *toro* was *anovillado*, young and of noble heart, and the matador on his mettle, the killing was *cuaja*, beautiful and clean. I was in awe of the matador's nerve in this dance of death, and cognizant of the cruel edge that underlay the crowd's pleasure and my own when killing was dressed up for show. I didn't mind the blood.

But I'm longing to see the elusive tusked whale up close, sunlight sparking on its marbled skin, the curvy, heart-shaped flukes. Alive is what I want. Not dead. Not the beach turned to abattoir. Not yet. I imagined I was ready for anything.

How do I straddle these two distinct worlds? What does it mean to watch killing for food when I'm not acquainted with the hunted? How do I think that loin of pork ends up on my plate, for heaven's sake; that far from hunting what we eat, we grow animals for slaughter? I feel like a hypocrite.

I try to imagine the hunter's rush of adrenalin, a cool eye lining up the harpoon with the moving target, the dangerous chase, the elation when the strike goes home. That takes me part-way there, but Barry Lopez gives me another way to think about the hunt when he writes, "The blood ... is a sign of life going on, of other life going on. Its presence is too often confused with cruelty."

It is my good fortune to be in this place at this time, in the Inuit story. On the campsite there are three hunters and a teenage son. A narwhal has just been cut into slabs and cached in a circle of stones, waiting to be taken by outboard motor back to Qaanaaq, where, as tradition dictates, it will be shared. The narwhal's crimson stain has been sucked out to sea by the tide. The kayaks are cradled again on the rocks, harpoons, lines, float and drogue meticulously returned to their proper places on the deck. I ask the young man if he knows how to kayak. He ducks his head shyly and says "No."

The old ways are going. The ice is going. Without ice, without the hunt, *we will be nothing*, says Jens from Qaanaaq.

After the event,
I will remember how water pours out its heart
into all the empty places. The mountain can't say *no*,
nor ice defend its frozen symmetry. After all,
brother ice and sister creek are still exploring the world.
One morning a fulmar circled
dove
spreading ripples
in its own wing-tipped liquid mirror.

How does the wet mosaic meet the white-capped cliff
or become highway to humans
inside the fields of ice?
A sea whose fire is mixed with glass
might be Nekivik's version from the veranda
of her strong-held house on the booted ocean floor.
There, knives of sunlight slit the black water
where shrimp-crackle and leviathan-clicks
unravel the wires of silence: cacophony
under the current
                                        wave chop and winding weather
                                                                                going on.

I have lived inside the weather,
filled my belly from the creek's curly beard,
so cold it makes my teeth ache –
and how the doting light loves a water drop
                                                                        pendulous
on the lip of summer –
                                                ice's catch and release game
– like Nekivik stealing the seals –
before and after freeze-up.
I will keep returning to the centre
of earth and gravity,
my heart relaxed by the eloquence
of tall white words.
                                            Now I am left with the land
for bedrock: a dream of light;
the avian perfection of a poppy petal's flutter;
ice's tender turquoise skirts
improvising a history of water.

Note:

ULTIMA THULE

Around 325 B.C., the seafarer Pytheas of Massalia discovered an island, six days sailing north of England, which he called Thule. It is generally thought that the island was present-day Iceland. At that time Thule meant the northernmost known island. But with increased geographical knowledge the name eventually moved farther north. The farthest north: Ultima Thule. Thule became synonymous with cold wilderness.

In 1910 Knud Rasmussen established the Kap York Trading Post. On a suggestion from the manager, Peter Freuchen, it was called Thule. The trading post financed the famous Thule expeditions.

Archaeological investigations at the Eskimo settlement of Uummannaq, in the vicinity of the trading post, introduced the name Thule into Eskimology in 1921 as a term for the youngest Eskimo culture, whose people came to Greenland around the year 1200 – the Thule culture. The Thule people were the founders of today's Greenlanders.

In 1963 the area was given official status as the 17th municipality of Greenland – the Thule municipality. The northernmost community in the world.

Bibliography:

BROWNING, ROBERT. Introduction to *The Divine Comedy • 1 Hell.* Translated by Dorothy L. Sayers. Penguin Classics, 1949.

BRUEMMER, FRED. *The Arctic.* Optimum Pubs., International. Montreal, 1982.

BRICK: A LITERARY JOURNAL. "Eleanor Wachtel: In Conversation with Hugh Brody." Issue 68, Fall 2001.

COUSINEAU, PHIL. *The Art of Pilgrimage: The Seeker's Guide To Making Travel Sacred.* Conari Press, 1998.

EHRLICH, GRETEL. *This Cold Heaven: Seven Seasons in Greenland.* Pantheon Books, New York, 2001.

FREUCHEN, PETER. *Book of the Eskimos.* Edited and with a Preface by Dagmar Freuchen. The World Publishing Company. Copyright 1961.

ELIOT, T. S. "The Dry Salvages." *Four Quartets.* Faber and Faber, 2001.

HAINES, JOHN. "News from the Glacier." *Selected Poems 1960-1980.* Wesleyan University Press, Middletown, Connecticut, 1982. *Other Days: Selections from a Work in Progress.* Graywolf Press, Port Townsend, 1982.

HERBERT, WALLY. *Hunters of the Polar North.* Time Life Books, 1981.

HOSS de le COMTE, MÓNICA GLORIA. *The Tango.* Maizal Ediciones, 2000.

LEE, DENNIS. *Body Music: Essays.* Anansi Press, Toronto, 1998.

LOPEZ, BARRY. *Arctic Dreams: Imagination and Desire in a Northern Landscape.* Bantam Books, New York, 1986. *About This Life: Journeys on the Threshold of Memory.* First Vintage Canada Editions, May 1999.

McKAY, DON. *Vis à Vis: Fieldnotes on Poetry & Wilderness.* Gaspereau Press MMI, 2001.

MOWAT, FARLEY. *Polar Passion.* McClelland and Stewart Ltd, 1967.

NUTAAQ MEDIA INC. & NATIONAL FILM BOARD OF CANADA. *Broken Promises, The High Arctic Relocation.* Director, Patricia V. Tassinari. A video, Toronto Public Library.

PIELOU, E. C. *A Naturalist's Guide to the Arctic.* The University of Chicago Press, Chicago and London, 1994.

RAFFAN, JAMES. *Tumblehome: Meditations and Lore from a Canoeist's Life.* A Phyllis Bruce Book. Harper Collins Publishers Ltd, Toronto, 2001.

RASMUSSEN, KNUD. *Intellectual Culture of the Iglulik Eskimos.* Vol.1. Translated by W. Worster from Danish original. Pub: New York: AMS Press, 1976.

RICHLER, NOAH. *This Is My Country, What's Yours? A Literary Atlas of Canada.* McClelland & Stewart Ltd, 2006.

RILKE, RAINER MARIA. "*Sonnets to Opheus.*" II, 23. *The Selected Poetry of Rainer Maria Rilke.* Edited and Translated by Stephen Mitchell. Vintage International Edition, 1989.

RUMI. "The New Rule." *The Essential Rumi.* Translations by Coleman Barks with John Moyne. HarperSanFrancisco, 1996.

SERVICE, ROBERT. "The Law of the Yukon." *The Best of Robert Service.* McGraw-Hill Ryerson, 2001.

SHAKESPEARE, WILLIAM. *The Works of Shakespeare.* Hamlet, Act I, Scene II. Oxford University Press, 1955.

The Faber Book of Exploration. Edited by Benedict Allen. Faber and Faber, 2002.

Acknowledgments:

This book is for Carol, whose steady presence in my life gives me courage.

The poem on page 34 was previously published by *The Fiddlehead.*

I wish to thank my brother Arthur, whose quick red pencil made the first incisive marks on an early version of the manuscript.

To Ruth and Igor Lugenbuehl for consultation.

Thanks to Bruce Meyer for giving me direction.

To Donna Langevin who recommended me.

To my publisher Richard Grove, who invited me to add poetry to the prose.

I am indebted to my editor Allan Briesmaster, whose high standard helps me live up to myself.

About the Author

In the author's own words, "Living on the cusp of my personal frontiers is a recurring theme, and in my writing I conduct a conversation with the land, seeking to understand my place in the larger order, and in the power and fragility of nature. I consider myself an explorer, charting the serendipitous events where the physical and the miraculous meet. I am interested in the authentic moments, when we forget ourselves and find that we have come home."

Rosemary Clewes has made six trips to the Arctic in both winter and summer. She has rafted some of the great rivers in the Yukon and Alaska, and kayaked in eastern Arctic waters, camping on both Greenland and Ellesmere Island. She has reached the highest latitudes by icebreaker.

Her extensive northern travels are forming a body of work in both poetry and prose. Works in progress include: "Once Houses Could Fly," a long poem describing a two week kayaking trip in the Kane Basin of the east coast of Ellesmere Island; and "The Woman Who Went to the Moon," about one week in January in the mid-Arctic community of Igloolik, where the Rising of the Sun Ceremony is celebrated after four months of darkness. Many of her poems have been published in literary journals. A crown of sonnets on two weeks kayaking in Greenland was nominated by *The Malahat Review* for the National Magazine Awards in 2006. She won a first honourable mention in *Arc Poetry Magazine*'s 10th Annual Poem of the Year Contest and she was a finalist in the 2006 CBC Literary Awards.

Rosemary Clewes was born in Toronto and has a list as long as your arm of her many passions. Alongside her work as an MSW, a Gestalt and Marriage and Family Therapist, she was an accomplished horsewoman, painter and printmaker. Now she writes poetry, practices the piano, and travels by icebreaker to the ends of the earth in search of home.